Praying the Truth

Praying the Truth

Deepening Your Friendship with God through Honest Prayer

William A. Barry, SJ

LOYOLA PRESS.
A JESUIT MINISTRY

Chicago

LOYOLA PRESS.
A JESUIT MINISTRY

3441 N. Ashland Avenue
Chicago, Illinois 60657
(800) 621-1008
www.loyolapress.com

Imprimi potest: Very Reverend Myles N. Sheehan, SJ, provincial

Unless otherwise noted, the Scripture quotations contained herein are from the *New Revised Standard Version Bible: Catholic Edition*, copyright © 1993 and 1989 by the Division of Christian Education of the National Council of the Churches of Christ in the U.S.A. Used by permission. All rights reserved.

The quotations from *The Spiritual Exercises* are taken from *St. Ignatius of Loyola. Personal Writings*. Tr. and Ed. Joseph A. Munitiz and Philip Endean. London, New York: Penguin Books, 1996.

"Wild Gratitude" by Edward Hirsch is from *The Living Fire: New and Selected Poems*. New York: Alfred A. Knopf, 2010.

Parts of chapters 10 and 15 originally appeared in *Human Development*. Permission to reprint is gratefully acknowledged.

Parts of chapter 16 originally appeared in *Catholic World*. Permission to reprint is gratefully acknowledged.

Cover art: © Yevgen Timashov/moodboard/Corbis

Library of Congress Cataloging-in-Publication Data

Barry, William A.
  Praying the truth : deepening your friendship with God through honest prayer / William A. Barry.
      p. cm.
  Includes bibliographical references (p.).
  ISBN-13: 978-0-8294-3624-2
  ISBN-10: 0-8294-3624-3
1. Prayer--Catholic Church. I. Title.
  BV215.B372 2012
  242—dc23

                                                                    2011037336

Printed in the United States of America
11 12 13 14 15 16 Versa 10 9 8 7 6 5 4 3 2 1

Dedication

To the staff of Campion Residence and Renewal Center
with admiration and great gratitude

Contents

Preface

This book is the third in a series of books that explore the metaphor of friendship as a way to understand and to engage in the relationship God wants with us. *A Friendship Like No Other* gave indications from Scripture that God desires our friendship, and it explored some of the implications of using this metaphor for our lives as Christians. In *Changed Heart, Changed World* I looked at how engaging in friendship with God changes our world for the better. In this book I explore how our friendship with God transforms personal prayer.[1] I hope to help readers engage more confidently with God in the kind of conversation the best of friends have with one another. I put the book in your hands with great hopes that it will enable you to enjoy talking with God as friend to friend.

As usual, I am grateful to many friends who have been willing to read my drafts and provide helpful feedback. Robert J. Doherty, SJ, Daniel and Patricia Farrell, Meghan Farrell-Talmo, Kathleen Foley, SND., Robert J. Gilroy, SJ, Francis J. McManus, SJ, James Martin, SJ, and William C. Russell, SJ, provided this gracious service for this book and helped me greatly, especially when my confidence faltered. Vinita Wright of Loyola Press gave invaluable suggestions on how to make the book more accessible.

My provincial superior, Myles Sheehan, SJ, read the manuscript in one day and gave it a thumbs up; he continues the encouragement to write I received from previous provincials. Paul Holland, SJ, my local superior during most of the writing of the book, and his successor, Robert Levens, SJ, gave me strong support. God has blessed me in my superiors.

In this book I tell stories of people I know, many of them through spiritual direction. I thank all of them for entrusting me with their experiences of God and for giving me permission to use these stories (altered to preserve anonymity).

During the writing I reached my eightieth year of life and my sixtieth as a Jesuit. My annual eight-day retreat in the summer of 2010 was a chance to thank God for all the blessings of my life. Prominent were my parents, my sisters and extended family, the Sisters of Mercy who taught me in grammar school and the Xaverian Brothers who taught me in high school, and the priests of Sacred Heart parish in Worcester, Massachusetts, who nurtured my earliest religious longings. Since I was staying at the College of the Holy Cross for my retreat, I was able to visit the cemetery where my Jesuit teachers are now buried and to thank them personally for all that they did to help me grow as a Christian and as a writer. Going over my years as a Jesuit gave me countless reasons to thank God for many Jesuit friends over the sixty years. Some periods stood out, among them my five years in Ann Arbor at the University of Michigan, where I was nurtured as a psychologist and writer by so many friends in the Psychology Department and as a religious by the community of priests and sisters who were studying alongside me during those eventful years. I thanked God with great joy for the years at Weston Jesuit School of Theology in Cambridge and especially for the colleagues who cofounded and developed the Center for Religious Development as a training center for spiritual directors; the work we did together at the Center has colored the rest of my life.

Remarkably at this stage of my life I find myself as happy as I have ever been. It is remarkable since, for the past fourteen years, I have lived at Campion Center in Weston, Massachusetts, which is a renewal center and a retirement and nursing home to elderly Jesuits of the New England province who now devote themselves to serving God by praying for the Church and the Society of Jesus. The center is a large operation in an equally expansive building. Needless to say, the center could not operate without a rather large nursing, maintenance, janitorial, and kitchen staff and other personnel. Rather amazingly, in spite of its size and its diversity, Campion Center is a house of warmth, cheer, and love. Surely the fact that the Jesuits who are assigned to the nursing facility take seriously their mission to pray and to help one another in ways that are very touching contributes to this atmosphere; I admire them very much and am immensely grateful to them for helping to make this present stage in life one of my happiest. But the staff, by their generosity, their care for the elderly Jesuits, their extraordinary kindness and cheerfulness, their prayerfulness, their humor, and their love, make the atmosphere of the center possible. Many of these dedicated men and women are immigrants who work two jobs to help their families back home and who suffer when they suffer. I salute all the staff and gratefully dedicate this book to them.

May God be praised forever!

1
Prayer as Relationship

Why pair truth telling with prayer? Let me tell you how the book came about.

I believe that God wants a personal relationship, an adult friendship, with each of us and that prayer is the best way of engaging in that friendship. By prayer I mean what occurs when I am conscious in some way of God's presence. So prayer can be as simple as watching a child trying to speak words, looking at sunlight glancing off snow-covered trees, playing with your dog, feeling the wind on your face, hearing birds sing, smelling bacon sizzling in a frying pan, looking at someone you love; all can be prayer if you're aware of God's presence as you take in these experiences.

Prayer can be as simple as "Help me" when I am down in the dumps or "Wasn't that lovely" when I am delighted by a friend's call to wish me well, as long as I am consciously saying or thinking these words to God. Prayer can happen when I walk in the woods, admiring the natural beauty and fierceness of what I notice, while aware that I am walking with the Creator of these woods. Prayer covers a wide territory in my view. All that is required is that I am conscious of God's presence in whatever activity I engage.

Ignatius of Loyola is known for wanting to find God in all things—that is, to be able to do all things while, at the same time, being conscious of God's presence. In other words, he wanted to be prayerful all the time. A tall order, you might say, but Ignatius believed that a person could come close to this with the help of God and by the regular practice of paying attention to what happens in daily life. He could hope for such a state because of his Christian belief that God, the creator of the universe, is never absent from any part of this universe. Hence, whether we are aware of it or not, we are always in God's presence no matter what we are doing.

Prayer, as conscious relationship, is the royal road to finding God in all things and to a deeper friendship with God. That's what this book is about. We grow in friendship with another human being by becoming more and more transparent with each other, as we will see in a little more detail in chapter 2. What I mean by truth telling is covered by the word transparency, but I want to spell out in the book what this means concretely for you. Here I want to mention some of the recent experiences that have inspired me to write about this topic.

For Lent of 2010 I decided to ask God every day: "What do you want for our friendship?" Almost as soon as I began to focus on this question, I felt God's love for me, and then experienced some tangible examples of that love both in prayer and in daily life. I took these experiences as God's response. Then my prayer took its usual route of distractions about worries or things to do; when I noticed this and turned back to God, I said something like this, "There I go again." God seemed to reply,

"Why don't you talk to me about these distractions." When I did, I noticed how the concerns evaporated; moreover, I often knew how to approach, in a more positive and less self-absorbed way, what I was going to do or the people I was concerned about. When I began to talk to God about my distractions, they were no longer distractions; they became openings to dialogue and greater transparency with God.

A woman whom I see for spiritual direction told me about her frustrations with a work situation. I asked her if she had spoken to God about these frustrations. She said she had, but it hadn't helped; she just got more frustrated and angry. I asked her how God responded to her frustrations. She answered, "I know that he listens and that he will be present." I said, "I didn't ask what you think, but how God responded." She pondered and realized that she didn't know for sure; she presumed God's response. Again I noted that we were not talking about her presumptions but about God's actual response. As our conversation continued, she became aware of the difference between dialogue and monologue and of how much better she felt when she spoke the truth to someone, including God, and felt heard, even if there were no immediate solutions to her worries and concerns.

A rather scrupulous man in spiritual direction continually brought up his concerns about others' anger or possible anger at him. He often went to great lengths to avoid people who might get angry with him. Prayer was often a time to mull over these situations and people and to ask God to help him cope with them. Finally one day it seemed to click that he could just tell God how he felt about these people and situations and see how God responded. At that point he told me that he felt at home with an imagined scene of Jesus with Martha and Mary and that he could tell them more of the truth of what he was experiencing. There were tears of relief in his eyes.

A final example came from another spiritual-direction session around the same time. A professional social worker was dealing with a very painful illness in his family, an illness that seemed to be getting worse by the day. Until recently he had been able to cope and had felt the consolation of God's abiding presence with him and his family. But this week he had felt very angry at the person who was sick and angry and despairing about their situation. Instead of telling God how he felt, he went out and had a few drinks to relieve the tension. Later when he reflected on what had happened, he realized that this crisis had brought him to a point where he discovered another facet of himself to reveal to God, namely his anger and despair. So he resolved to open this side of himself to God.

These experiences catalyzed some ideas that had been percolating for a few years about the psalms as prayer and about how we grow in friendship. I had thought of writing a book using the Psalms, or selected psalms, as examples of transparency, or truth telling, before God. The psalmists "let it all hang out" in prayer. They often speak the unspeakable to God, and yet throughout the centuries the book of Psalms has been considered a model for prayer—a model not often followed in practice.

So I intend to engage in a conversation with you about what it might mean for your prayer life to engage in a friendship with God, a friendship God wants very much. To grow in that friendship, you and God will have to become more and more transparent with each other; you and God will have to tell the truth to each other. In the process, I believe, you will find yourself slowly transformed.

2
Prayer and Friendship

Let's look at how friendships grow. I invite you to think of a good friend and keep that friend in mind as you ponder the following paragraphs.

Honesty: The Bedrock of Friendship

In Richard Russo's novel *That Old Cape Magic* Jack Griffin and his old friend Tommy are back together again in Hollywood after Jack's separation from his wife. After a paragraph describing how careful they were with each other, each avoiding noise or questions that might disturb the other, Russo writes: "They were, that is, careful, as if consideration and not honesty was the bedrock of friendship."[2] Russo gets it right. Honesty is the bedrock of friendship. Whenever we sense that we are walking on eggshells with a friend, we know that the friendship is in trouble because we are skirting some sensitive issue that makes it difficult to be honest with each other.

Friendship develops through mutual honesty, through truth-telling or transparency, doesn't it? I'm convinced that the friendship God wants of us and offers to us develops similarly. At the Last Supper in John's Gospel, Jesus says to his disciples and to us:

> You are my friends if you do what I command you. I do not call you servants any longer, because the servant does not know what the master is doing; but I have called you friends, because I have made known to you everything that I have heard from my Father. You did not choose me but I chose you. And I appointed you to go and bear fruit, fruit that will last, so that the Father will give you whatever you ask him in my name. I am giving you these commands so that you may love one another.
>
> —John 15:14–17

Notice that Jesus says, "I have called you friends, because I have made known to you everything that I have heard from my Father." He has gone all out in truth telling with them and us. He is hoping that we will reciprocate that honesty. Does this make sense to you? Are you intrigued? Then read on.

Job Placement Is Not God's Primary Interest

In the introduction I mentioned my 2010 Lenten practice of asking what God wanted in our relationship. One day God seemed to be telling me, "Most of the time when you ask me what I want from you, you're looking for something to do for me. I don't want you to do anything for me; I want you to be my friend, to let me reveal myself to you and for you to reveal yourself to me. The things-to-do will take care of themselves." In my usual distracted way, I went off on tangents such as how this would be interesting for the book, but God kept coming back to the same theme. At one point I was reminded that I had written of God's vulnerability; God seemed to say, "This is an example of my vulnerability. You and so many others continue to talk to yourselves about what I'm like, but you don't give me a chance to reveal myself to you. So you often get me wrong."

I am trying to put into words what came to me in this period of prayer. I did not hear a voice saying what I put between quotation marks; I am presenting the gist of what I gleaned from the conversation. As I reflected on it, it seemed to ring true to God. I do not believe that I was deluding myself.

Have you ever experienced something like this? Perhaps you were talking to God about something important to you, say your sick child, and felt that you were not alone in your concerns, that God was also concerned about your child and about you. It's that kind of feeling that I refer to when I say that God responded. Once a man I know was very angry at God because of the loss of his parents at an early age, and he told God, in no uncertain terms, how angry he was about that. I asked him how he felt after that angry prayer. He said that he felt better, that he had been heard and accepted. These are the kinds of experiences I refer to when I talk about listening for God's response. Later we will discuss how to decide whether what you experience is really from God or not.

What Is Prayer?

Let's reflect on my "conversation." God really does seem much more interested in a real friendship than in job placement. In other words, God is not so much interested in giving me marching orders as in our friendship. In addition, I draw from this "conversation" that for God friendship seems to come down to mutual self-revelation, to telling the truth about ourselves to each other.

How do you understand prayer? Take some time to reflect on what you do when you pray.

What I do too often is *say* prayers, such as the "Our Father" or "Hail Mary." I'll say a prayer without much attention and at the end hardly know what I have said or that I was talking to anyone. Or I tell God how sorry I am for what I have done, but the words are almost by rote, without much emotion or attention. Or I start to tell God about things that concern me but then begin to think of solutions to the problems or make up dialogues with the people I'm concerned about or upset with. I realize that most of my "prayers" are really monologues; I'm talking to myself and figuring out what God's response might be. Does this description of "prayer" ring a bell with you?

You'll have noticed that God "said" to me, "You and so many others continue to talk to yourselves about what I'm like, but you don't give me a chance to reveal myself to you." God is not all that interested in monologues or in requests for a job description; God wants a conversation between friends, a conversation that includes listening as well as talking on both sides. So, for God, prayer is a dialogue, not a monologue.

Getting Started

How do we get started in this dialogue with God? Well, here's what I do now. I look for some place where I won't be too distracted. Most times it's our house chapel. But you can try your kitchen table as you have your morning coffee, your living room if no one else is there, or a nearby church or chapel. You could also take a walk in the woods or in a park.

After I'm settled in the place, I recall that God is waiting for me to pay attention, is looking at me, as Ignatius of Loyola wrote in his *Spiritual Exercises* (n. 75).[3] I ask God to help me pay attention, to pull me out of my self-absorption. Then I ask

God for what I want; for example, in the 2010 Lenten period I asked God to let me know what he wants of our relationship. After this, I try to focus my attention on God—Father, Son, and Holy Spirit—and let things unfold. Sometimes I find myself having the kind of dialogue that I described earlier, but not in just that way. It seems as though these thoughts come to me, and I know what I am experiencing is different from when I am talking to myself.

I mentioned asking God for what I want during this time of prayer. It helps focus a conversation to know why you want to be with the other person. So pay attention to what you want from God each time you begin to pray. Imagine Jesus saying to you what he said to the two disciples of John the Baptist when they approached him, "What are you looking for?" (John 1:38). What is your spontaneous response? Start with that desire until some other desire arises.

Notice that Jesus is asking them a personal question, "What do *you* want?" They can answer only if they are honest. In the story they blurt out, "Rabbi, where are you staying?" It's kind of superficial, but Jesus invites them to come and see. Thus begins their journey of friendship with Jesus. Perhaps you want to know that Jesus cares about you. Well, tell him that directly and wait to see what happens.

Prayer is a rather simple thing when you get down to it. It's just two friends hanging out with each other, sharing thoughts and feelings, asking and giving forgiveness, asking and giving advice. Prayer is what happens when two friends are together and are aware of each other's presence. You probably already know a lot about it. My suggestions may just encourage you to trust what you are already doing for prayer.

The Art of Listening

It's not easy to listen to another. When the other person starts talking, we begin to think of how we will respond. Conversation for many of us consists of keeping the ball in the air, not in really paying attention to the mind and heart of the one speaking. If I enter the conversation with the idea that I have to do my part to keep the conversation going, then I may be using at least half my mind and heart trying to work out my next conversational move. I am not listening well.

Also our own self-concerns get in the way of listening well. For example, my friend starts talking about her backache; I start thinking of my own back pain and tell her, "I know how that is" and begin to talk about my bouts of back pain. Or I may tell her what helped me or someone I know and advise her to do the same. She may not get the chance to talk about how much this pain has changed her life and her mood.

Sometimes, too, a friend starts telling me about some deep pain and sadness, which reminds me of my own unwelcome moods or of my occasional feelings that there is no light at the end of the tunnel. I want to get off this topic as soon as possible. So I try to encourage my friend, telling him that these moods are only passing. Thus, I prevent my friend from telling me his whole truth. Perhaps he only wants to be heard.

The art of listening well is not learned easily, even by those whose profession requires it. It was difficult for me to learn to listen when I was a fledging psychologist and later a beginning spiritual director. In both cases I was often too concerned about how I would respond to the other person to listen well and, as a result, often missed the deeper emotional impact of what the other person was trying to tell me. We so much want to help that we are unable to listen well. What helped me was supervision as both a psychologist and as a spiritual director; I discovered how my own anxieties got in the way and gradually I was weaned from needing to know the right responses. One day I found myself really listening to the other person, felt captivated, even honored, by what was being communicated and the trust the other person was showing, and then was able to communicate that I was in tune with the other. And I did this without trying hard. After that I was able, generally, to give up my need to have answers or even conversational gambits to keep the conversation going. However, the need to solve problems dies hard. To this day I can feel ill at ease if someone leaves a session of spiritual direction without a solution to some deep problem. *Where have I failed?* lurks in my psyche.

Our culture seems to believe that every problem is solvable with enough ingenuity and good will. So if someone presents a problem to us, we may feel that we have not done our job by just listening to that person with compassion. I have come to believe that just listening with empathy and compassion is a much needed capacity in our world, one in much too short supply. Yet, I have come to believe that this capacity is God's greatest power and one that God wants us to emulate for the sake of the world. In spite of what we often are led to believe, God is not a problem solver, a Mr. Fixit. God has promised us nothing more than friendship, and on my better days this is enough for me.

Listening to God

Now insofar as we have problems listening to another human being, we will have problems listening to God. After all, according to Jesus, the love of God shows itself in our love of our neighbor. And listening to our neighbor without concern for ourselves is one sign that we truly love that neighbor. So if we cannot do this with our neighbor, we cannot do it with God. I have found that learning to listen to others well has gone hand-in-glove with being able to listen well to God.

Throughout the book you will find examples of how God has communicated with me and with others. In every case those who have "heard" God communicating have, at least for that moment, been able to be in the present and to forget their own concerns. For example, a man wrote to me that he would be "walking and talking to God, telling God how hard it is still with my father's death, and noting the consolation that comes almost immediately." In the present he tells God what he is feeling and experiences healing. A woman who is a hospital chaplain had had a very hard day, as had the doctors and nurses in her unit, because of the deaths of five young patients. She got a call to come to the unit to help the staff talk about the pain they had just endured. She felt overwhelmed and angry. As she walked toward the unit, she started yelling at God, telling him how angry she was and that everyone was asking too much of her. As she walked into the unit, one of the nurses said, "Here's D, a breath of fresh air." Recently she had read an article that compared compassion to oxygen. She felt overwhelmed with the presence of God and very grateful that God had let her embody compassion for this staff. This woman was present to her own pain and her anger and told God about it and almost immediately felt God's response through the nurse's comment on seeing her.

A young priest told me that one time he was in a chapel and felt a strong love for God and told God, "I love you." Almost immediately he felt God saying, "I love you too." In that moment he felt overwhelmed with joy, gratitude, and a feeling of great well-being. Almost as immediately, however, the thought came, *How do I know this is God? I could be kidding myself.* When he first told me of hearing God's response, he only recalled being afraid and asking the question. Only when I asked him to recall the experience did he realize that the question had driven out the memory of his joy, gratitude, and feeling of well-being. In the moment of telling God, "I love you," he was totally present and thus was able to experience God's response. But in a split second he lost that sense of the present and began to doubt what had just happened, and, of course, he lost contact with God.

We listen to God, I believe, when we are caught up in present reality, not worried about the past or the future. In that reality we encounter more than what is present before our eyes; we also sense a Presence that quickens our hearts and gives us hope and courage. And this sense of God's presence in present reality can come in odd and even horrible events. When she and everyone else sensed that she was dying, Julian of Norwich heard these words: "All shall be well and all manner of thing shall be well."[4]

How Do I Know I'm Hearing God?

"How I can be sure that what I hear is really from God?" That's what this young priest asked me. I, too, had asked that question about my own prayer experience. Here's how I decided. After that period of prayer, I reflected on what had happened. I noticed that during the times I later wrote out as God's response I was focused and could easily recall afterward what had happened and what God seemed to be revealing. Moreover, I was rather excited by what was happening. I felt that God and I were really present to each other and that I was being led toward a deeper relationship with God. And what I "heard" rang true to what I already deeply knew about God and myself. These times of prayer felt something like the experience of reading a novel or poem or even a book on prayer and thinking, *That's right on the money; it rings true to life.* In addition, I felt eager to return to prayer the next day.

In contrast, I noticed that when I was off on tangents, I was talking to myself or engaging in imagined conversations with others or with a reader, and it was hard to remember what had just happened in the preceding few seconds or minutes. I was also unfocused, my mind wandering all over the place, and when I came to, as it were, I realized that I was not conversing with, or listening to, God. It was something like how I have felt after reading a boring novel, a poor poem, or a theoretical book on prayer; it didn't ring true to life. And I was not eager to continue such prayer.

Because of these different experiences I concluded that the parts of the prayer that ended up in quotation marks were from God, the others not. Because of such experiences I have a fairly good antenna for knowing when my prayer is real and when it is not. Does that make sense to you?

When I helped the young priest decide whether what he had heard was from God, I pointed out the same criteria. I asked him what would happen if he had continued to enjoy the experience of God's love. He realized that he would be focused on God and not on himself or on questions, and that he would have what he most deeply wanted: closeness to God. The doubts and questions pulled him away from God, not toward God. And these doubts and questions were not seriously looking for answers. Their whole purpose, it seemed, was to keep him self-absorbed and in doubt, a sure sign that the one Ignatius of Loyola calls the enemy of human nature is up to his usual tricks (*Spiritual Exercises*, n. 10).

God wants our friendship, and this friendship is like our human friendships, which thrive on mutual trust and honesty. God wants to reveal as much as possible to us and asks the same from us. We deepen our friendship with God by opening ourselves more and more honestly to God in prayer. The ideal is to be totally transparent with each other. Ignatius of Loyola, at the end of his *Spiritual Exercises*, expresses this ideal in the "Contemplation for Attaining Love."

> Point 1. This is to bring to memory the benefits received—creation, redemption, and particular gifts— pondering with great affection how much God Our Lord has done for me, and how much He has given me of what He has; and further, how according to His divine plan, it is the Lord's wish, as far as He is able, to give me Himself; then to reflect and consider within myself what, in all reason and justice, I ought for my part to offer and give to His Divine Majesty, that is to say, everything I have, and myself as well, saying as one making a gift with great love:
>
> "Take, Lord, and receive all my liberty, my memory, my understanding, and my entire will, all that I have and possess. You gave it all to me; to you Lord I give it all back. All is yours, dispose of it entirely according to your will. Give me the grace to love you, for that is enough for me."
>
> —*Spiritual Exercises,* n. 234

It's rather poignant, isn't it? God wants to share everything with us but cannot, both because we are not God and because we resist receiving God's self-revelation. And God wants us to share everything we are, to be totally transparent and trusting. The prayer "Take, Lord, and receive . . ." expresses that ideal. I hope that we can together move toward this ideal as I write this book and as you engage in this friendship into which God invites you.

3
How Secrecy Poisons Friendship

In the last chapter I cited Richard Russo's comment that honesty, not consideration, is the bedrock of friendship. In this chapter I want to reflect on how poisonous secrecy can be to friendship, and even to sanity.

The Dangers of Secrecy

One of the slogans of Alcoholics Anonymous is: "We are only as sick as our secrets." At the end of many meetings the leader of the day asks, "Does anyone feel the urge to drink today?" This gives those close to "falling off the wagon" a chance to say publicly that they have the urge and thus gives them the opportunity to get support. The spiritual discipline of A.A. asks members to let others know when they are in danger of taking the first drink. Many of the twelve steps are, in fact, part of the spiritual discipline of becoming more transparent so that we can continue to turn our unmanageable life over to God and become sane. Secrecy threatens an alcoholic's sanity.

Sanity means that we are in touch with reality. For an alcoholic, the reality is that he or she cannot drink responsibly, cannot control the impulse once the first drink is taken. Following the urge to keep secrets may lead back to the insane notion that the alcoholic can drink responsibly.

I believe that the same kind of secrecy threatens our sanity quite apart from substance addiction. When I was a psychotherapist, it often became clear that some secret shame or event lay behind the neurotic behavior of a client. Sometimes the event was so traumatic that it had been blocked from consciousness, making it a secret even from the person it had affected. But sometimes the event or secret was known to him or her, and the effort to keep it secret brought on or exacerbated the neurotic or self-defeating behavior.

As we learn more about the recent sexual-abuse crisis in the Roman Catholic Church, it seems that some church leaders felt that they had to protect the reputation of the church or religious congregation by trying to keep secret the horror of sexual abuse of children and teenagers. This brought disastrous consequences for those abused, for the abusers, and for the very institutions they wanted to protect. In retrospect they might conclude that what looked like a sane approach was actually out of touch with reality. Perhaps you remember instances in your own life when secrecy led to behavior that was out of touch with reality.

Have you ever noticed what happens when a family or community is unwilling to address important issues? Communities of a religious congregation can gradually become like the caricature of the English men's club, where no one dares say or do anything that will upset the routine even when the routine includes some strange and unhealthy behavior by some of the members.

One would be hard-pressed to see in such a community a gathering of friends of Jesus.

I have also seen how the inability to confront the elephant in the living room can reduce a family to formality and exaggerated politeness. Everyone knows that June is chronically depressed, for example, or that Joe is a problem drinker, but no one dares say or do anything to address the situation. Perhaps some of the others whisper amongst themselves about the situation, but nothing is done to deal with the problem. Mind you, politeness is better than rampant violence, but you would not see as ideal a family in which politeness and consideration reign over honesty and deep friendship. Vibrant communal life is characterized by honest conversations not only about the outside world, but also about the interactions of the community members.

This being said, we must remember that truth telling can get out of hand. Twelve Step programs presume that what is said in meetings will be held secret by those in attendance. If you want to reveal your alcoholism, that's one thing, but no one else has the right to make revelations about your alcoholism. Sometimes truth telling can be a cover for savage personal attacks. In the United States, at least, there is an unhealthy desire to ferret out the secrets of public figures to their detriment. It is very difficult for a public figure to have a private life away from reporters and cameras. And the willingness of some people to air their worst secrets on talk shows and "reality" television smacks of exhibitionism. Finally, there are secrets that must be kept, even from our closest friends, because they have been entrusted to us by people who expect that we will not tell anyone.

Do we have to tell our friends everything? Of course not. But if I have a secret that is bothering me while I am with a close friend, that friend will sense something awry. I can, at least, tell my friend that something is bothering me, something I can't talk about, something that has nothing to do with us. This will clear the air, at least if my friend is a true friend.

Shame and Secrecy

What prompts the secrecy that is harmful to sanity and to friendship? Most often, it's shame. At an A.A. meeting, those with an urge to drink may be ashamed to say so, feeling that others will think poorly of them. A sponsor for other alcoholics may be ashamed to admit the urge in their presence for fear of losing authority with them. If I feel that alcoholism or depression is shameful, I may find it very hard to name the reality in one of my family or community members and try to help him or her.

The feeling of being ashamed can come from a number of sources. People can be ashamed of their bodies; for instance, ashamed that they are overweight or underweight, too short or too tall, not the right shape or color. In our oversexed culture women can be ashamed of their breast size, men of the size of their penis. Some are ashamed that they were born poor and had limited schooling; others that their parents were divorced or were caught up in a scandal. I'm sure that you can add to the list.

No matter what it is that makes us ashamed, we try to keep it secret, even from our best friends. In Russo's novel *That Old Cape Magic,* Jack Griffin is ashamed of his parents and tries to keep his wife, Joy, from being drawn into what he considers their condescending way of dealing with others. When his mother calls, he takes the telephone into another room so that Joy will not hear. But his parents do intrude into the marriage because they intrude into Jack's psyche all the time, and Joy feels excluded from an important part of Jack's life. The secret poisons their relationship. I don't want to spoil a good read by saying more about this fine novel, but Russo knows that honesty is the bedrock of friendship.

When a topic that touches on our shame comes up in conversation, we're very likely to bring the interchange to a halt. Often in such circumstances conversation becomes more narrow in range because so many topics touch upon the shame of one or the other. Conversation can become rather banal and uninteresting to everyone involved. Secrecy can poison the growth of a friendship.

The Burden Is Lifted

What happens when we tell the secret about which we are ashamed? When people at an A.A. meeting admit that they have an urge to drink today, the urge seems to lessen and other members of the group reach out to thank them for their honesty and to offer help. A woman told me what a relief it was to tell people at an Al-Anon meeting how she was actually feeling. For the first time in her life she said what she really felt and was listened to with empathy and understanding. Just telling the truth in such a setting is life-giving. This kind of truth telling goes on all over the world in a variety of Twelve-Step meetings. People tell the truth and find their way back to sanity from their addictions or from the ravages of a loved one's addictions and discover the capacity for friendships of depth.

Secrecy and Friendship with God

Some of the things we are ashamed of can get in the way of friendship with God as well. Friendship with God develops gradually. First you notice that you are attracted to God, and you desire to know more. As you get to know God's generosity in creating the world and you, you find yourself excited and eager to pray. After a while, however, you begin to wonder, *This is fine for holy people, but can it be true for me?* You remember the things you are ashamed of. You think, *God knows everything. So he knows that I am (a homosexual, the child of divorced parents, someone who cheated on exams, or whatever it is). I'm crazy to think that God would want my friendship.* At this point you might be tempted to withdraw from prayer, sensing that you are unworthy of God's friendship. But notice that in the scenario I have described, you have not spoken openly with God about what causes you shame.

You might want to say, "But God already knows everything about me. I don't have to tell him what I am ashamed of." It's not about the information God might have; it's about whether you will trust God enough to say what is on your heart and mind and wait for a response. You are not worried about what information God has, but about God's reaction to the information. So, just as with a friend, the only way forward is to take the risk of telling God and seeing if the friendship is still on. What is at stake is the developing friendship with God. Notice that in my scenario, you were tempted to stop praying because you felt unworthy.

If you don't tell God what you are concerned about, your relationship will become more and more formal and, to be frank, boring. Once I found myself rather bored during some spiritual-direction sessions with a priest. When I reflected on my boredom, I realized that before this I had looked forward to his visits; so I wondered what was going on. Since we had a very good relationship, I indicated that I was finding our conversations rather boring. It turned out that he was not praying because something had come up that he was ashamed to mention to God. As with any friend, the issue is one of trust, trust that God really is interested in friendship with "the likes of us," that is, with us who have all kinds of warts and moles and shameful things that make us feel unworthy of God's—or perhaps anyone's—friendship. If we don't take the chance of being honest, we won't really grow in friendship with God or with anyone else.

God Breathes a Sigh of Relief

When people are honest with God about the shameful things in their past or present, they may sense that God breathes a sigh of relief. "Finally, you got that off your chest. Now we can move on. Thanks for the trust." They may not hear it in these words, but in the sense of relief they themselves feel. They have let the cat out of the bag, and the sky has not fallen. They may also sense something like this from God: "I made you out of love; nothing you can do will change that love. You're gradually getting the hang of who I really am." We have been given back a bit of sanity.

Sanity, you see, consists in feeling in my bones that God loves me, warts and all, and that nothing I do will change God's love for me. It is insane to feel that God's love depends on me in any way. When I hesitate or refuse to tell God things that I consider shameful because I feel unworthy of God's friendship, I am making myself the arbiter of who God is; God, in other words, is, for me, someone who does not like the kind of person I am. That really is insane, isn't it? When we begin to feel God's unconditional love and to trust it, we begin to believe in God, not in some idol of our own imagining. So sanity, faith, and friendship with God go hand in hand, and they are abetted by truth telling.

I hope that you agree with me that secrecy can be injurious to friendship, because, if you don't, the rest of the book will not make sense to you. I believe that friendship with God rests on some of the same bedrock as any friendship. We deepen our friendship with God by a self-revelation that gradually weans us from the secrets that bind us and frees us not only for a deeper friendship with God but also for abundant life (cf. John 10:10).

4
Telling God about Your Attraction

The first movement toward friendship happens when I am attracted to another person and take the chance of showing that attraction in some way. It is a moment of vulnerability, but it's a necessary one if any friendship is to get off the ground. The person making that initial move is vulnerable because there's the chance that the other person will not be interested in pursuing the friendship.

We know that God has already taken the first step in vulnerability; God created us for friendship, and we can reject the offer. We make our first step when we find ourselves attracted to God and express that attraction. Have you ever told God that you are attracted, that you want this relationship? What would it be like to do so?

Are You Attracted to God?

I believe that all of us are attracted to God. In any person there is a welling up, every so often, of a sense of great well-being and a desire for "we know not what." It can come upon us at the oddest times, but most often it happens when we are momentarily caught off guard and then really pay attention to something that faces us. I have found instances of such desire in novels and detective stories, in autobiographies—even of agnostics—in poetry, and in conversations with ordinary people.

Once I was staying alone in a house on the seashore. At dinner time I was stunned to see the full harvest moon rise from the sea. I went outside after dinner and walked along the beach. The moon was so bright that I could see my shadow as I walked. Then I noticed how the moon silvered the waves as they quietly broke on the beach. Lines of silver came and went as I walked along. I felt a surge of great well-being and desire. The desire was not only to continue to see the beauty before my eyes, but for something much more. I felt immensely grateful to God for this moment. Later the English Benedictine Sebastian Moore gave me the words to describe the desire I felt; it was the "desire for I knew not what," for the Mystery we call God.[5] The beauty of that evening had captivated me enough that I forgot my petty concerns for a while and realized how much I was attracted to God who creates this lovely world and gave me a glimpse of his artistry.

I believe that God's desire creates us and keeps us in existence. God is always trying to draw us into a deeper friendship. When we are surprised by something like that moonlit evening, we feel this desire of God and our own deepest desire to respond to God's desire. Perhaps you recall such experiences in your own life.

"My Soul Thirsts for You"

A number of psalms express a deep desire for God, for example: "As a deer longs for flowing streams, / so my soul longs for you, O God" (Psalm 42:1). Psalm 63 is even stronger:

> O God, you are my God, I seek you,
>   my soul thirsts for you;
> my flesh faints for you,
>   as in a dry and weary land where there is no water.
> —Psalm 63:1

The psalmist's heart is an open book before God; he does not hesitate to express his deep attraction to God. He knows the thirst of a person caught in the desert and compares his desire for God to that thirst. Later he describes the satisfaction of his desire for God as a rich feast. His desire is so great that he never wants to forget God.

So we are encouraged to let God know how attracted we are, and we can do it in whatever way seems most true to our experience. For the psalmist, desert thirst seemed most like his desire for God. You can express your desire for God in your own words.

If we realize that our very existence depends on God's desire for us, it makes it easier to respond in kind. Our desire for God is only a pale reflection of God's desire for us.

As you try to express your attraction to God, you might be helped by this prayer of my friend John Carmody, written a few weeks before his death from multiple myeloma:

> You give us two commands
> and let them merge into one.
> We are to love you with all our heart
> and to love our neighbors as ourselves. . . .
> I love you, God, and have for all my adult life.

I love you badly, distractedly, impurely,
but from the first I knew what your name meant,
first received the slightest inkling,
I knew you were all I needed or wanted
and my life gained purpose and order.
What shall I return to you
for all the favors that loving you has brought me?
I shall dwell in the thought of you,
the hope for you,
the trust in your care for me,
and the love that you pour forth in my heart
all the days of my life
and all your heaven to come.[6]

What an honest, heartbreaking expression of longing for God from a dying man! "I love you, God, and have for all my adult life. I love you badly, distractedly, impurely, but . . . I knew you were all I needed or wanted." Each of us can say that, if we love God at all, it is badly, distractedly, and impurely. John Carmody told God the truth, both about his attraction and his ambivalence. We can do the same.

5

Telling God about Your Fears

It's hard to admit, even to friends, that we are afraid of something. This may be truer for men than for women, but if it's true of you, this chapter may help.

When you are with a friend and are riddled with fear, what else do you have to talk about that's important? If you don't talk about what's uppermost in your mind—the fear—you probably have little of substance to say. Also, you won't be fully attentive to what your friend is saying to you. This is just one more way that honesty—or the lack of it—affects our relationships.

If you open up about your fears, chances are, your friend will listen and sympathize. Once this happens, you feel a great change. Now you're not so alone. And you're relieved to have spoken aloud about the fear. Often it feels as if a burden has been lifted—and this happens when we're honest about our fears to another human being! It has been my experience—and I have witnessed this in other people, too—that opening up to God about our fears leads to great relief.

Stories of Fearful Prayer

You would not expect to hear a warrior king express fear, but in Psalm 55 the great King David does tell God his fears and in detail.

> My heart is in anguish within me,
>   the terrors of death have fallen upon me.
> Fear and trembling come upon me,
>   and horror overwhelms me.
> And I say, "O that I had wings like a dove!
>   I would fly away and be at rest;
> truly, I would flee far away;
>   I would lodge in the wilderness;
> I would hurry to find a shelter for myself
>   from the raging wind and tempest."
>
> —Psalm 55:4–8

David trusts God enough to say that he wants to run away and hide—and would if he could. Later he becomes more specific about the source of his anguish and fear. He says that he could bear the taunts of his enemies, but what terrifies him now is the treachery of a friend. Often we find that telling one truth or part of the truth leads to further truth telling. Then finally he can say:

> Cast your burden on the Lord,
>   and he will sustain you;
> he will never permit
>   the righteous to be moved.
>
> —Psalm 55:22–23

As a result of this outpouring of fear and anguish, David seems to have derived comfort. If you are filled with fear, you can take David as an example and tell God what you fear and tell it in detail. As you do this, you might find that you are more able to face your fears honestly and in the process become less fearful.

Once I was quite anxious and not even sure what I was anxious about, and I could not get to sleep. I tried my usual techniques to get quiet, to no avail. Finally, I took my own advice to others and began to tell God how I was feeling. It soon became clear that I was afraid of losing a friend because of a misunderstanding. As I continued to talk to God, I realized that I was overreacting to the situation; my anxiety lessened, and I fell asleep.

On one occasion Jesus and his disciples, some of whom were seasoned fishermen, were in a boat on the Sea of Galilee when a sudden storm arose.

> On that day, when evening had come, he said to them, "Let us go across to the other side." And leaving the crowd behind, they took him with them in the boat, just as he was. Other boats were with him. A great wind-storm arose, and the waves beat into the boat, so that the boat was already being swamped. But he was in the stern, asleep on the cushion; and they woke him up and said to him, "Teacher, do you not care that we are perishing?" He woke up and rebuked the wind, and said to the sea, "Peace! Be still!" Then the wind ceased, and there was a dead calm. He said to them, "Why are you afraid? Have you still no faith?" And they were filled with great awe and said to one another, "Who then is this, that even the wind and the sea obey him?"
>
> —Mark 4:35–41

If ever you feel really terrified, remember this scene. You are not alone. Just call out to Jesus and see what happens.

God's Response

A friend of mine told me of a brutal confrontation he had with a supervisor, a confrontation that left him frightened, practically cowering afterward. He began to tell Jesus how he was feeling, and after a time he had an image of Jesus standing behind his supervisor, telling my friend that he could learn something from this event. As he reflected on the encounter and this prayer experience, he did learn something about himself that gave him consolation.

On another occasion, the same man was overwhelmed with fear after a very hard meeting with his employer that threatened his job, his livelihood, and even his identity. He felt totally alone and helpless. Again he began to pray for help, overwhelmed by a sense of total loss. As he prayed, he felt that he was in a whirlwind and that everything he held dear was being torn away from him. It was terrifying until, finally, in the darkness and loneliness he sensed a light and felt comforted by the presence of God, a God who would never abandon him no matter what else he lost.

Whenever we are afraid, we can turn to God in deep trust, describing in detail what troubles us. Recall the words of Jesus, "So I say to you, 'Ask, and it will be given you, search, and you will find; knock, and the door will be opened for you. For everyone who asks receives, and everyone who searches finds, and for everyone who knocks, the door will be opened'" (Luke 11:9–10).

Fear of God

Some people are more afraid of, than attracted to, God. How can they proceed? It's too easy to say, "Tell God you're afraid." You can tell a friend you're afraid of her only if you have some trust that she will not bite your head off. After all, to tell a friend you're afraid of her makes you even more vulnerable. So, if you are afraid of God, you might first take some time to reflect on a time or times when you trusted God, when you felt safe in God's presence. If you can recall such a time, you can then tell God that you wish you still had such trust, still felt safe. Then you might be able to tell God why you are afraid.

I gave a talk once at a university, about prayer as personal relationship. Afterward a professor said, "I want to have a closer relationship with God, but I know that if I do get close, God will ask something of me and I'm afraid of that request." I blurted out, "You can tell God exactly what you just said." He said, "Can I tell God that?" to which I responded, "It's a relationship; so you can tell God anything that you're feeling."

No matter what it is that makes you afraid of God, you can say it, trusting that God will be pleased that you are telling the truth. In Mark's Gospel the rich man who could not give up his wealth went away sad. But he could have just told Jesus, "I can't do that; can I still hang around with you?" The sad thing is that he walked away rather than admit his fear of losing his riches (cf. Mark 10:17–22).

Whenever you feel afraid of God, remember Jesus' encouraging words: "Come to me, all you that are weary and are carrying heavy burdens, and I will give you rest. Take my yoke upon you, and learn from me; for I am gentle and humble in heart, and you will find rest for your souls. For my yoke is easy, and my burden is light" (Matthew 11:28–30). God has come close to us in Jesus; there is nothing to fear from him.

6
Telling God about Your Successes

Usually when something good happens to us, we want to tell a friend, unless, of course, we are inhibited for some reason. How often do we think of telling God? Not often, at least if I take myself as normative. But perhaps this could be one of our first thoughts if we took friendship with God seriously.

Let's look at the story of the seventy disciples who were sent out on mission by Jesus (Luke 10:1–24). When their mission was over, the "seventy returned with joy, saying 'Lord, in your name even the demons submit to us!'" (v. 17). Notice that, though they give Jesus himself credit, they still are eager to tell Jesus what *they have done*: "the demons submit to *us*." They know that it was in Jesus' name that they cast out demons, but this knowledge does not remove the joy they have that the demons submitted to them. Jesus, it seems, wants to underline both aspects of their joy because he replies,

"I watched Satan fall from heaven like a flash of light-ning. See, I have given you authority to tread on snakes and scorpions, and over all the power of the enemy; and nothing will hurt you. Nevertheless, do not rejoice at this, that the spirits submit to you, but rejoice that your names are written in heaven."

—vv. 18–20

The Mutuality of Friendship

To exist at all, let alone to do anything good or useful, we depend at every moment on the creative and sustaining desire of God. For the disciples this meant that it was by the power of God that they had overpowered the demons. But this truth does not remove another, namely that the disciples did act with power over the enemy. Clearly, for Jesus, the disciples and he are in the mission together; the disciples, too, are necessary for the success of the mission. Luke goes on to describe Jesus' joy and exultation.

At that same hour Jesus rejoiced in the Holy Spirit and said, "I thank you, Father, Lord of heaven and earth, because you have hidden these things from the wise and the intelligent and have revealed them to infants; yes, Father, for such was your gracious will. All things have been handed over to me by my Father; and no one knows who the Son is except the Father, or who the Father is except the Son and anyone to whom the Son chooses to reveal him."

Then turning to the disciples, Jesus said to them privately, "Blessed are the eyes that see what you see! For I tell you that many prophets and kings desired to see what you see, but did not see it, and to hear what you hear, but did not hear it."

—vv. 21–24

If the disciples had felt inhibited in telling Jesus how happy they were about their successful mission, they might not have had this chance to hear Jesus' own joy at what they had done in his name.

Inhibitions

But often we are inhibited from talking about our successes, even with friends. Sometimes we hesitate because we are afraid that the friend will become jealous of our success or will feel inferior to us. Or perhaps he or she will dismiss the success as not that important or meaningful. Sometimes we fear seeming proud of our accomplishments. Sometimes we are held back by the memories of past hurts, situations in which we tried to talk about our successes but received cold, critical, or angry responses. For example, you got a raise at work and told a friend, who said, "It's not much of a raise." So there are a number of possible sources for hesitation to tell a friend about your successes.

We may hesitate to talk about success because we live in a competitive world where often enough my gain can seem to be your loss. One of the presumptions seems to be that there is not enough to go around. Even success seems to be measured out. There is only one valedictorian at most graduations, one P.G.A. winner; one Super Bowl winner. It can seem as though if I win, you must lose. Success for one person must mean failure for another.

But this is not God's economy. Because of God's generosity there is room for every human being to do well, to succeed, to enjoy abundant life. The more we act in light of God's great generosity, the more we live under the assumption that there's enough for everyone, the freer we will be to talk about success—and the more we will free others to do so.

There is no reason to hold back on telling God about our joys, our excitement, our successes in life. We are not in competition with God. God does not look upon us as rivals. In fact, by telling Jesus about their joy, the disciples gave Jesus a chance to rejoice with them and to teach them something about his relationship with his Father and about God's economy.

An Example from the Psalms

Some of the psalms are occasioned by joy or success either of the psalmist or of the people. For example, Psalm 87 glories in the city of Jerusalem (Zion). Perhaps it was sung at a civic celebration of Jerusalem as God's city. Of course, the psalmist attributes the successes of the city and of its people to God, but obviously he is also pleased with the glory of the city itself as a sign of the people's success.

> On the holy mount stands the city he founded;
>   the Lord loves the gates of Zion
>   more than all the dwellings of Jacob.
> Glorious things are spoken of you,
>   O city of God. . . .
>
> And of Zion it shall be said,
>   "This one and that one were born in it";
>   for the Most High himself will establish it.
> The Lord records, as he registers the peoples,
>   "This one was born there."
>
> Singers and dancers alike say,
>   "All my springs are in you."
>
> —Psalm 87:1–3, 5–7

Clearly the psalmist is proud of Jerusalem. He is proud that people talk of the illustrious people born there, that the city is renowned in surrounding, even enemy, lands. As he recounts these glories, he does not forget that God's favor has made them possible. Perhaps telling God of his pride in his city has kept him aware of the truth that all depends on God. But he still tells God of his pride.

Is there anything comparable in your life? Maybe you just received the alumni/ae magazine from your old school and read that one of your classmates won a Pulitzer Prize in journalism and another was honored by the state for her work with the homeless. You feel proud to be from this school. You could tell God how you feel and note how God responds to you.

Your own success at some venture could be a topic, or the joy you have in the success of a friend or family member. It's another way, and a rather easy one, to tell the truth to God. Such prayer keeps us grounded in reality, namely in our utter dependence on God, and thus leads easily into a prayer of gratitude.

7
Telling God about Your Sadness

Telling God about our joys and successes is rather easy. It's another matter to tell the truth about our sad moments. All of us get down at times. Think of some time when you have felt down in the dumps, ill at ease, sad, even depressed. Did you try to tell a friend how you were feeling? If so, what happened?

If your friend listened with sympathy and compassion, you were fortunate indeed. Often when we try to tell others, even friends, how sad we are, they want to give advice, remind us that others are worse off, or tell us their own troubles. Many people, I believe, are poor listeners, like a bishop who, in a homily to his priests, admitted that as soon as someone began to tell him some problem, he started to think of solutions. It's not easy to find someone who really listens. Sometimes we have to tell our friends that we just want them to listen, not to offer advice right away. And sometimes our friends need to remind us to do the same.

Telling a Friend

Part of the distress of sadness comes from the feeling that no one understands or wants to understand. The fact that most people in our culture seem unable to listen with sympathy to those who are struggling often reinforces this feeling. Sadness, especially deep sadness, is often accompanied by the feeling of being alone in a black hole from which there is no escape. The friend who listens with sympathy shows that he or she is not afraid of being sucked into that hole. Having some company gives us hope.

The psalmists must have found that God was such a listening friend. Take, for example, Psalm 6.

> O Lord, do not rebuke me in your anger,
>   or discipline me in your wrath.
> Be gracious to me, O Lord, for I am languishing;
>   O Lord, heal me, for my bones are shaking with
>   terror.
> My soul also is struck with terror,
>   while you, O Lord—how long? . . .
>
> I am weary with my moaning;
>   every night I flood my bed with tears;
>   I drench my couch with my weeping.
> My eyes waste away because of grief;
>   they grow weak because of all my foes.
>
> —Psalm 6:1–3, 6

This is a lament about a grave illness and a prayer for recovery. The psalmist seems to believe that God has let him suffer this illness to discipline him. He begs God to be gracious instead. No matter his belief about the source of his illness, he still tells

God how he is feeling, and in concrete details: "my bones are shaking with terror." He is not afraid to take God to task, "while you, O Lord—how long?" "Turn, O Lord, save my life; deliver me for the sake of your steadfast love" (v. 4). In other words, he asks God to be true to their friendship. He tells God about his night terrors in some detail and with strong emotional language. And finally, it seems, he feels heard and vindicated.

> Depart from me, all you workers of evil,
>   for the Lord has heard the sound of my weeping.
> The Lord has heard my supplication;
>   the Lord accepts my prayer.

—vv. 8–9

Psalm 13 is another example.

> How long, O Lord? Will you forget me forever?
>   How long will you hide your face from me?
> How long must I bear pain in my soul,
>   and have sorrow in my heart all day long?
> How long shall my enemy be exalted over me?
>
> Consider and answer me, O Lord my God!
>   Give light to my eyes, or I will sleep the sleep of death,
> and my enemy will say, "I have prevailed";
>   my foes will rejoice because I am shaken.
>
> But I trusted in your steadfast love;
>   my heart shall rejoice in your salvation.
> I will sing to the Lord,
>   because he has dealt bountifully with me.

The psalmist laments God's absence while under attack from enemies. Four times, in quick succession, he cries out, "How long?" and demands some relief from his pain. In effect, he says that it is unacceptable for God to forget him and leave him to the mercy of his enemies. And, just as in Psalm 6, the psalmist seems to find relief as a result of his prayer of lament.

But God Knows Everything—Why Do I Have to Tell Him?

These are good examples of how to let God know of your sadness. And don't let the thought that God already knows how you feel get in the way. The psalmist is aware of God's knowledge. It's not a question of knowledge but of friendship. A friend may well know that you are sad, but she will feel trusted if you tell her about it. And you will feel a lot better. Friendship with God operates much the same way. God is interested in your willingness to entrust how you are feeling. So when you are sad or depressed, take a moment to become aware of God's presence, of God looking at you. Then tell your story in detail. Don't be afraid to let it all spill out, even your anger at God for letting things happen to bring you to this state.

Gerard Manley Hopkins, the great Jesuit poet of the nineteenth century, was no stranger to sadness and deep depression. He had studied theology and knew that God is all-knowing. Yet he not only took the time to tell God in detail what he was going through but also spent even more time working out his lament in this poem.

> I wake and feel the fell of dark, not day.
> What hours, O what black hours we have spent
> This night! what sights you, heart, saw; ways you went!
> And more must, in yet longer light's delay.
>
> With witness I speak this. But where I say
> Hours I mean years, mean life. And my lament
> Is cries countless, cries like dead letters sent
> To dearest him that lives alas! away.

I am gall, I am heartburn. God's most deep decree
Bitter would have me taste: my taste was me;
Bones built in me, flesh filled, blood brined the curse.

Selfyeast of spirit a dull dough sours. I see
The lost are like this, and their scourge to be
As I am mine, their sweating selves; but worse.

On June 25, 1883, six years before his death of typhoid, Hopkins wrote to his friend Robert Dixon: "I see no grounded prospect of my ever doing much not only in poetry but in anything at all. At times I do feel this sadly and bitterly, but it is God's will. . . ." None of Hopkins' poems saw the light of day during his lifetime, and during his last years, which he spent as a teacher in Dublin, he suffered not only from the weather and the obtuseness of his students but also from being away from his family and his beloved England. At times he also felt the absence of God, as evidenced by the lines "cries like dead letters sent/ To dearest him that lives alas! away."

Hopkins did not shy away from telling the truth to God. In this and other poems he let God know the deepest secrets and agonies of his heart, even his near despair. And he could complain, as in another dark sonnet, to God and to Mary, "Comforter, where, where is your comforting?/ Mary, mother of us, where is your relief?"[7] We do not have to hedge our bets with God; we can say everything to "dearest him" even though God may seem to live far away. It seems that Hopkins found some solace through communicating to God his deep anguish. But that solace was no cheap grace, as we know from his poems of lament and darkness.

God's Comforting Presence

In my experience, people who can tell God their sadness and distress usually sense that God is listening with compassion and understanding. In chapter 3 I mentioned a man who wrote how he often was "walking and talking to God, telling God how hard it is still with my father's death and noting the consolation that comes almost immediately." He realizes that God cannot change the reality of his father's death, but the fact that he feels heard with compassion and love gives consolation and hope. People who talk to God this way are enabled to go on, as Hopkins was. It is, however, a hard lesson to learn because we have to give up an image of God as Mr. Fixit. Those who have been willing to speak to God the truth of their darkness, sadness, and near despair find that the deeper friendship they now enjoy is ample reward for giving up that false image.

An example of such honesty with God comes from the diaries kept by Etty Hillesum, the Dutch Jewish writer, during her last years in Amsterdam before being deported to Auschwitz where she was executed in a gas chamber. Published as *An Interrupted Life: The Diaries, 1941–43*, the writings show how she developed a profound relationship with God in those dark times. Repeatedly she tells God what is going on in her heart and mind, honestly revealing her weaknesses as well as her strengths. In one entry she tells God how anxious she is and ends with these words: "I am beginning to feel a little more peaceful, God, thanks to this conversation with You."[8] Like Hopkins, she seems able, because of her honesty with God, to laugh and enjoy life in spite of the hellish darkness that surrounds and eventually kills her.

I am not advocating that prayer take the place of other means of dealing with deep sadness and depression. They may also require the help of a physician or a counselor. Friends are also a help, if they are willing to listen with a compassionate heart. I do want to emphasize that talking with God as friend to friend can be greatly consoling and life-giving. I hope that I have given you some ways of approaching God as a friend when you do experience dark times.

8
Telling God about Your Pettiness

If you have never felt envious of others, you are lucky indeed. Most of us can't say that. Much of the advertising industry seems predicated on the belief that envy is everywhere. We are presented with people who are better looking, more prosperous, and happier than we are in order to entice us to buy the products that have made them so superior. Envy fuels much of our economy. And one influential theory about violence argues that we learn to desire things through imitating others; because they want something, we want it and will even resort to violence to get it. Envy may be something that affects you. Are you willing to admit that to God?

It's not easy. None of us likes to admit that we are envious of others. It makes us feel small-minded and selfish. "I should be happy, not envious, that others, especially my friends, are happy. What would my best friend think of me if I told her that I was

envious of her?" We don't want to seem petty and selfish in others' eyes. However, if we are truthful, we would have to say that
we often are petty and envious of others. Can we tell God?

Psalm 73

The psalmist has had a serious realization.

> Truly God is good to the upright,
>   to those who are pure in heart.
> But as for me, my feet had almost stumbled;
>   my steps had nearly slipped.
> For I was envious of the arrogant;
>   I saw the prosperity of the wicked.
>
> For they have no pain;
>   their bodies are sound and sleek.
> They are not in trouble as others are;
>   they are not plagued like other people.

—vv. 1–5

You could almost imagine that he's been watching American
television's exaltation of the well-to-do. Do you recognize yourself as you read these lines? If you were feeling this way, would
you start to pray as he has done? After this beginning he goes on
to tell God how arrogant and violent these people are, and yet
they prosper and enjoy a good reputation. Then he says:

> All in vain I have kept my heart clean
>   and washed my hands in innocence.
> For all day long I have been plagued,
>   and am punished every morning.

—vv. 13–14

Have you ever felt like this—that you have done all the right
things but have nothing to show for it? Well, the psalmist is

willing to tell God the truth of what he is feeling, in effect saying, "I do everything right and get nothing but pain for it." Now notice what happens, seemingly as a result of his honesty.

> When my soul was embittered,
>   when I was pricked in heart,
> I was stupid and ignorant;
>   I was like a brute beast towards you.
> Nevertheless I am continually with you;
>   you hold my right hand.
> You guide me with your counsel,
>   and afterwards you will receive me with honor.
> Whom have I in heaven but you?
>   And there is nothing on earth that I desire other than
>   you.
> My flesh and my heart may fail,
>   but God is the strength of my heart and my portion
>   forever.
>
> —vv. 21–26

He seems to have come to some peace with his situation as a result of his honesty with God. He realizes that God is with him, and that's enough. His envy seems to vanish in the course of this very honest prayer.

Go and Do Likewise

Envy is only one of the many less than pretty features of our inner landscape. We are also spiteful, self-absorbed, and self-pitying. We can become angry with a sick spouse or friend just for being sick—angry when a spouse who is terminally ill and in great pain wants to die or when a friend with Alzheimer's disease keeps repeating the same question. When we become aware of such pettiness, we don't like ourselves. But how often does such dislike lead to a change of heart? Not often, as far as I can see. Mostly, when I bemoan my failures to be the kind of person I would like to be, it leads only to self-flagellation, not to a change of heart. These features of my inner landscape remain entrenched. And the self-flagellation keeps me self-absorbed. Even though I am now attacking myself, the focus is still on me. The enemy of human nature could not be more pleased. Nothing changes, and the focus stays on me, not on God. Does this ring true for you? We could learn a lot from imitating the psalmist.

He told God the truth: he was envious of the wicked because they seemed to prosper while he did not. When he turned his pettiness into prayer, something positive happened; his focus shifted from himself to God. As a result, he came to some peace and, we presume, a change of his inner landscape. I have found that telling God the truth about such feelings and asking for help to move beyond them changes my focus from myself to God and, in the process, leads to inner transformation. By the grace of God I become less envious, less petty, less full of self-pity.

Over and over again we discover that telling God the truth, no matter how unsavory that truth is, pulls us out of self-absorption and folly and moves us toward becoming the images of God we are created to be.

9
Telling God about Your Anger and Rage

Have you ever felt that you were being put upon by life or by other people undeservedly? You got cancer even though you took care of your health, watched what you ate, never smoked. You were falsely accused of something and could not convince people of your innocence. Your spouse died suddenly, and you are left alone to take care of the children and all the details of life. *Why me?* you might quite reasonably have felt. Did you think of telling God how upset you were?

"Why Do You Sleep, O Lord?"

The psalmists told God that what happened to them wasn't fair. Psalm 44 is a fine example. In it the psalmist expresses his own and the nation's lament after they had suffered a terrible defeat. In the first stanza the psalmist tells God what the people have heard of God's past deeds on their behalf. In the second stanza he notes that they had always boasted that God had enabled them to defeat their enemies. Then the psalm takes a turn toward complaint.

> Yet you have rejected us and abased us,
>   and have not gone out with our armies.
> You made us turn back from the foe,
>   and our enemies have gotten spoil.
> You have made us like sheep for slaughter,
>   and have scattered us among the nations.
> You have sold your people for a trifle,
>   demanding no high price for them.
>
> —Psalm 44:9–12

Just as earlier he had ascribed the victories of Israel to God's hand, now he says that it's God's fault that they suffer so grievously. One might expect that he will now go on to say that Israel has lost God's favor because of their sins, but that's not the way it goes at all. He tells God how undeserved their fate is.

> All this has come upon us,
>   yet we have not forgotten you,
>   or been false to your covenant.
> Our heart has not turned back,
>   nor have our steps departed from your way,
> yet you have broken us in the haunt of jackals,
>   and covered us with deep darkness. . . .
>
> Because of you we are being killed all day long,
>   and accounted as sheep for the slaughter.
>
> —vv. 17–19, 22

Then he seems to yell at God:

> Rouse yourself! Why do you sleep, O Lord?
>   Awake, do not cast us off for ever!

Why do you hide your face?
  Why do you forget our affliction and oppression?
For we sink down to the dust;
  our bodies cling to the ground.
Rise up, come to our help.
  Redeem us for the sake of your steadfast love.

—vv. 23–26

The psalmist insists that they do not deserve what has happened to them; they have been true to their covenant with God. In fact, they are suffering because of their fidelity to God. God is the one who has reneged on the covenant. And so the psalmist calls upon God to wake up and come to their rescue and reminds God of the "steadfast love" that has been God's hallmark in the covenant relationship with Israel.

If you ever feel that you have been unfairly treated by life, that you did all the right things and still had nothing to show for it, you can use this psalm as a model of how to tell God. You may, however, feel inhibited about doing so.

Sometimes we are hindered from expressing our resentment at life's hurts and disappointments, saying to ourselves that others have suffered worse or that God knows best. But, in fact, we do feel the resentment. It may show itself in a low-grade depression; I always seem to see the dark side of things and don't expect that things will ever get better. It may show in a resentment at others who have it better than I do; I can often come across as rather angry. And it may show up as a physical illness, such as an ulcer. I may continue to carry on my daily tasks and be a regular churchgoer, but I don't have much relish in my life. I may never take the time to tell God how I am feeling and find out that I am really resentful at the cards I have been dealt by life.

The psalmist gives us license to tell God exactly how we feel, even if we may cringe at expressing it so directly to God. It is a way of clearing the air between God and ourselves when such feelings arise. And it shows an enormous trust in God, our friend.

"You Are Like a Deceitful Brook"

When Jeremiah heard God's call to be a prophet, he said, "Ah, Lord God! Truly I do not know how to speak, for I am only a boy" (Jeremiah 1:6). Jeremiah told God the truth; he did not feel up to this call. God would have none of this, and Jeremiah accepted the call. Jeremiah did speak God's word to kings and religious leaders and was vilified, imprisoned, and threatened with death for doing so. He did not have a happy life. Some of his complaints to God are wrenching. I give two samples.

> You will be in the right, O Lord,
>   when I lay charges against you;
>   but let me put my case to you.
> Why does the way of the guilty prosper?
>   Why do all who are treacherous thrive?
> You plant them, and they take root;
>   they grow and bring forth fruit;
> you are near in their mouths
>   yet far from their hearts.
> But you, O Lord, know me;
>   You see me and test me—my heart is with you.
>   —Jeremiah 12:1–3

Jeremiah tells God how angry he is that the wicked prosper while he suffers. Many innocent people have suffered terribly. They have in Jeremiah a model of how to tell God of their anger and bitterness. In this text, Gerard Manley Hopkins heard complaints that enabled him to express his own anguish that none of his poems ever saw the light of day.

Thou art indeed just, Lord, if I contend
With thee; but, sir, so what I plead is just.
Why do sinners' ways prosper? and why must
Disappointment all I endeavour end?

Wert thou my enemy, O thou my friend,
How wouldst thou worse, I wonder, than thou dost
Defeat, thwart me? Oh, the sots and thralls of lust
Do in spare hours more thrive than I that spend,

Sir, life upon thy cause. See, banks and brakes
Now leavéd how thick! lacéd they are again
With fretty chervil, look, and fresh wind shakes

Them; birds build—but not I build; no, but strain,
Time's eunuch, and not breed one work that wakes.
Mine, O thou lord of life, send my roots rain. [9]

Modeling himself on Jeremiah, Hopkins tells God "I've spent my life for you, and you have treated me worse than an enemy would, though you are my friend." Have you ever felt this way? Could you speak to God this honestly? You might try it the next time you are feeling this angry.

Here is the second example from Jeremiah.

Your words were found, and I ate them,
   and your words became to me a joy
   and the delight of my heart;
for I am called by your name,
   O Lord, God of hosts.
I did not sit in the company of merrymakers,
   nor did I rejoice;
under the weight of your hand I sat alone,
   for you had filled me with indignation.
Why is my pain unceasing,

　　　my wound incurable,
　　　refusing to be healed?
　　Truly, you are to me like a deceitful brook,
　　　like waters that fail.

—Jeremiah 15:16–18

Jeremiah calls God a deceitful brook who makes fine promises but does not come through. Clearly Jeremiah was an angry man who railed against his persecutors and did not spare God from his anger and resentment.

How do you react to these prayers? Many cringe at the thought of saying things like this to God. But I believe that such prayers are examples of a close relationship. No matter how much the psalmist or Jeremiah rail against God, they never lose their trust and love of God. And, it seems, they felt God's love and trust in them.

Praying against Those Who Hurt Us

Have you ever been so angry at others that you wanted to hurt them in some way? If you can remember such a time, ask yourself whether you dared to tell God what you wanted. When I have felt such anger, prayer was the last thing on my mind or heart. I have yelled and cursed either aloud or in my thoughts, but I have not made such yelling and cursing into a prayer. Yet that's what Jeremiah and the psalmists do. They scream and curse in prayer about their enemies and sometimes they rage at God. Reflection on these prayers has led me to wonder about my own way of dealing with anger.

While my mind knows that anger is an emotion that comes upon me without my consent, my feelings don't agree. I feel ashamed when I have gotten angry and expressed it to another person, even when the anger is not directed at this person. My image of myself seems tarnished; I feel that others now see me in an unfavorable light and that I have sinned. My family upbringing had a lot to do with my reactions to anger and was abetted by a catechesis that made anger a sin to be confessed, especially anger at my sisters or my mother or father. So I have not been comfortable with the direct expression of anger to another, nor even with telling a friend how angry I am at someone else. Mind you, I do express anger, but I have never felt justified at being angry, even when there was good reason for the anger. I can confess past anger to God, but I find it very difficult to tell God how angry I am while I am feeling that way. Many of you may be in the same boat. But I am learning in my old age; so there is hope for us all.

Letting God Transform Us

Anger and aggression are part of our nature; we are created with fight-or-flight reactions to danger. Aggression, fueled by anger, is a gift of God that enables us to face danger. Hence our aggressive drive is among the things that God saw as "good" in creation. Moreover, anger at injustice can fuel efforts to right the wrongs. So my feeling reactions of shame and embarrassment about my anger are not in line with treasuring God's good gifts.

Anger is not, in itself, evil or sinful. But anger and aggression can lead to consequences that are not good for me or for others. I can hurt others, including the innocent, by outbursts of anger. I still cringe when I recall how in a fit of rage that welled up seemingly out of nowhere, I said some awful and hurtful things to a close friend. The shame and embarrassment that have kept me from letting God in on my anger have clearly not led me to a completely healthy use of anger and aggression. Perhaps writing this chapter is leading to some wisdom that might be helpful to all of us.

What has helped me is to tell God some of my angry thoughts and my resentments. For example, when driving, I can get quite angry at drivers who seem overly aggressive. I have gradually begun to let God know about these outbursts and to engage in such conversation closer and closer to the actual outburst. Often enough I do this with humor, "There I go again, as though I have never been aggressive," but nonetheless with honesty. I have noticed a gradual shift in my reactions as I drive; I seem to be getting less angry and aggressive. I have also told God about the kinds of behavior that get me angry, again with a gradual lessening of the anger, and sometimes with a different attitude toward the people who make me angry. So talking with God about anger, even with my inhibitions about showing anger, has had a positive effect.

I have not been able to tell God that I wanted people who have injured me to suffer. Yet, if the truth be known, I have wanted to hurt those who have hurt me. Jeremiah was able to tell God to take destructive action against his enemies. The psalmists, too, are able to tell God to do awful things to their enemies. The worst, for me, comes in the lovely Psalm 137 that begins:

> By the rivers of Babylon—
>   there we sat down and there we wept
>   when we remembered Zion.

—v. 1

It ends with these frightful lines:

O daughter Babylon, you devastator!
  Happy shall they be who pay you back
  what you have done to us!
Happy shall they be who take your little ones
  and dash them against the rock!

—vv. 8–9

The whole psalm is a lovely lament of a people in exile who feel unable to sing their songs in a foreign land, even though their Babylonian captors ask them to do so. Most of us, however, cringe at the last lines of this psalm. In the Liturgy of the Hours, when this psalm is used, the last stanza is removed, an indication of how uncomfortable the ending makes people. We have qualms, but clearly the psalmist had no qualms about saying what he felt to God. I wonder what happened after he said these last lines to God.

Notice that the psalmist tells God to take vengeance. Perhaps that prayer kept him from taking matters into his own hands and acting violently against his enemies. Another answer can be gleaned from Psalm 13. The psalmist complains angrily to God, demanding to know how long he must suffer, but then ends with these words: "But I trusted in your steadfast love; / my heart shall rejoice in your salvation. / I will sing to the Lord, / because he has dealt bountifully with me" (Psalm 13:5–6). Apparently telling God how angry he is has been helpful and led him to greater trust in God.

Stories of Angry Prayer

I recall a young woman, whose beloved father had died suddenly when the woman was a teenager, preparing for her wedding ceremony. (I have changed details to preserve anonymity but still give the gist of what happened.) One day, as she passed the church where the wedding would take place, she thought of the ceremony and of how her father would not be there to walk her down the aisle. Rage boiled up in her suddenly, and she began to rail against God for taking her father. She told God that she would walk down the aisle alone so that everyone would see how cruel he had been to take her father so early. She was surprised at how angry she was and at how straightforwardly she spoke to God. Afterward she noticed that she felt better. When I asked her how God seemed during this tirade, she said, "He listened; I knew that he was listening with sympathy. I felt that I had been heard." After that, she no longer seemed so interested in showing up God at the ceremony.

A few years ago Fr. Stephen Yavorsky, SJ, wrote an article about his difficulty in forgiving some Rwandans who had befriended him, he felt, in order to defraud the spirituality center in Kigali where he worked of large sums of money. When he realized that he had been cheated, he felt a murderous rage against these men, even thinking of ways to have them killed. One day he was praying and found himself in imagination on a cross next to Jesus on his cross. Jesus was about to forgive the people who had put him on the cross and who were jeering at him, when Yavorsky noticed that among the crowd were the men who had cheated him. He yelled at Jesus to stop, that these people did not deserve forgiveness. He found himself now among the crowd in front of Jesus. Jesus longed that everyone in that crowd join him on the cross of forgiveness, but Yavorsky could not do it. Then he was back beside Jesus; Jesus was begging him to join him in forgiving, but he could not do it. Finally, he was able to say to Jesus, "I'll look at you; you look at them." With that tiny admission he felt his heart begin to thaw. It took time, but gradually he was able to forgive the men who had cheated the center.[10]

A Jesuit told me that he once was so angry at another Jesuit that he wanted to hit him. He imagined Jesus sitting across from him and told Jesus how he felt; Jesus said, "Am I your best friend?" "Yes, of course." "Well, Joe is my friend." With that the Jesuit's attitude toward Joe shifted, even if only slightly at first.

Another Jesuit told me that he was once so angry at God that he said something like this: "You are God and you're bigger than I am. That's a fact, and you are going to win on this one. But let me tell you something: if I were you and you were I, I wouldn't do this to you." He felt relieved and rather comforted afterwards.

These stories illustrate what can happen when we speak honestly to God about our rage. If we are really engaging in a dialogue with Jesus, his attitudes will come through, and we will be faced with our need to change or to acknowledge our inability to change and to ask for help. I hope that the psalmist who wanted the Babylonians' babies bashed against rocks felt differently after telling God how angry he was at his enemies. It would not surprise me that the expression of such murderous rage to God and the realization of how God was listening would have brought a change of heart, at least over time.

If we are really talking to God, we can't help but take on some of God's own attitudes toward those who offend us. If I experience God listening to my rage, then gradually it will dawn on me that God loves my enemy as much as he loves me. Thus praying honestly about our anger and resentment seems to be transformative. But we will not be transformed if we do not let God know the truth about ourselves.

I think that writing this chapter has been a help to me to let Jesus in on my anger while it is erupting and to ask for help. I hope that it has helped you as well.

10
Telling God about Your Sexuality

"What does our sexuality have to do with friendship with God? As far as I can see, sexuality gets in the way of such a friendship." Not too many years ago I might have reacted this way. At the same time I might also have been intrigued by the title, hoping to find something helpful in dealing with my sexual urges. I hope that you are intrigued and that the chapter will help you overcome any hesitation you might have about bringing your sexuality into the friendship with God.

Take a few moments to reflect on how you have been doing with sexual issues in your life. Have you experienced sexuality as a gift or as a problem? What has been your experience of sexuality in relation with God? Have you ever talked openly with God about your sexual identity, your sexual impulses and fantasies, your sexual attractions?

Conflicted about Sexuality?

I suspect that many people are, like me, somewhat conflicted about sexuality. In spite of the sexual revolution that has transformed the landscape of most of the Western world in the past fifty years, many of us still are not really comfortable with sexuality, especially when sexuality is brought into contact with our relationship with God. Our ambivalence comes from many sources. How many of our parents welcomed our questions about the differences between girls and boys? How many were comfortable explaining how babies are made? Though as children we were naturally curious about everything, we quickly realized that sexuality was difficult, if not dangerous, territory. Religious education teachers often were just as uncomfortable talking about sexuality. In addition, religious teaching often presented sexuality as a minefield full of perils. When I was growing up, I never heard anyone in authority in church or school even hint at God's delight in creating us as sexual beings. Religious teaching on sexuality was about what not to do until marriage. Sexuality was more like a road to hell, it seemed, since any sexual activity outside of marriage was a mortal sin. So our knowledge of sexuality was minimal. We older folks did not grow up comfortable with issues of sexuality.

Since the sexual revolution of the 1960s, young people have had a different experience of learning about sexuality. What contact I have had with the younger generation leads me to believe that there is discomfort with sexuality among them, but that it has different origins and, perhaps, a different nature.

Younger people seem to know more about sexuality, and by "know" I mean that they have experiential knowledge. Statistics indicate that youngsters engage in sexual exploration much earlier than in my generation and, as a consequence, may be less uptight about discussing sexuality. Novels, movies, television, and other media give the impression that sexual expression is taken for granted when two people are attracted to each other. Yet young people are often hurt and bewildered by their experiences of sexual activity. I wonder whether as a culture we have found out what God intends with the gift of sexuality.

We have been discussing prayer as a way of telling the truth to our friend God and expecting the same from God. Someone might say, "Don't we tell the truth when we confess our sexual sins?" Yes, but that's not the kind of truth telling I mean here. I mean the same kind of truth telling that we discussed when we reflected on sadness and anger. Few of us, I believe, have tried to tell God the truth about our sexual orientation, desires, impulses, and fantasies and listened for God's response. Doing this, I believe, can be a great help, not only to our friendship with God, but also to our becoming comfortable with sexuality and more in tune with God's hopes for us.

The Song of Solomon

The psalms are no help here. There are no psalms that speak as frankly of sexual longing as they do of anger and sadness. The Song of Solomon or Song of Songs, however, gives us a clue that for biblical authors sexuality was not a taboo subject. If you have not read the book recently, do so now. It will help you realize that God is not an enemy of sexual attraction.

The Song is a series of often quite sensual and erotic love poems between a man and a woman interspersed with reminiscences and internal dialogues of the woman, dialogues between her and the women of Israel, and a few other poems. The lovers describe each other minutely and with graphic images, some of which may make us smile while others may arouse erotic and sexual feelings; these descriptions are sensual and erotic, teasing and flirtatious, but clearly fueled by ardent sexual attraction between the lovers. When I was in the Jesuit novitiate in 1950, we were not allowed to read this book of the Bible. You may understand why novice directors did not want mostly teenage novices to read this book!

You may also begin to wonder why this book is in the Bible, a question that has intrigued Jew and Christian alike over the centuries. The consensus of the tradition is that these love poems describe the covenantal relationship God wants with the people of Israel. While many modern scholars argue that the book is about the human, physical love between a man and a woman, Marvin Pope remarks:

> Nevertheless, the instincts and insights that from the beginning led both Christian and Jewish exegetes to relate the language of the Song to divine and superhuman love were based on internal evidence largely ignored by recent interpreters. . . . Sexuality is a basic human interest and the affirmation that "God is Love" includes all meanings of both words.[11]

Pope makes a strong statement, namely that the words *God is love* in the First Letter of John include all meanings of the words *God* and *love*. That means the sexual meaning of the word *love* as well. Let's try to take him seriously.

God's Passionate Love

In the Bible, outside the Song of Songs, there are strong statements of God's passionate, profligate love for the world, and especially for human beings, using language taken from human love. To a sinful, rebellious people God says, "I have loved you with an everlasting love" (Jeremiah 31:3); and, "Therefore, I will now allure her, / and bring her into the wilderness, and speak tenderly to her. . . . On that day, says the Lord, you will call me, My husband" (Hosea 2:14, 16). When the people said that the Lord had forgotten them, God replied, "Can a woman forget her nursing child, / or show no compassion for the child of her womb? / Even these may forget, / yet I will not forget you. / See, I have inscribed you on the palms of my hands" (Isaiah 49:15–16). The love and fidelity of God are described in terms of human passionate love. If, indeed, we are made in the image of God, then sexuality must have some reality in God. I hope that we can discover what this reality might mean by engaging honestly with God about our sexuality.

Getting a Start

How might we go about talking to God about our sexual desires, fantasies, and attractions?

First, be aware that God is with you, looking at you, waiting for *you* to become aware. You might tell God that you would like to become more comfortable talking about your sexuality and ask for help. If you are feeling any discomfort, just say so and see what happens. Do you feel a bit less nervous? Does God seem interested in knowing more about you? Remember that God made us sexual beings. Perhaps God wants us to share this aspect of our lives and help us live more fully and with more joy.

It might help if you remember that Jesus and his mother Mary had to come to terms with their sexuality as they grew into adulthood. Perhaps you can speak with Jesus or Mary more easily about your sexuality.

Now think of someone to whom you are attracted. Try to tell God what attracts you. You might start by describing the person, for example, giving details that you find attractive. Then you could describe the person's physical attributes that you find attractive. Just say whatever you can comfortably say. Do you get the sense that God is listening and interested? If you would like to know God's reactions to your attraction, ask, and wait for a response. Once again, you may not hear words, but you may sense something. Just pay attention to what goes on, and keep communicating.

If you are married, you might want to talk with God about your spouse and your sexual attraction to and activity with him or her. This might feel strange, but remember that your sexual union is part of the sacramental nature of your marriage. Try it and see what happens.

If you are single and are sexually attracted to someone, try telling God about your attraction, about how you feel in the presence of this person, about your dreams about him or her, and, as you get more comfortable in God's presence, about your sexual attraction. Try to be as concrete as possible. It might help to recall that God made you a sexual person with sexual desires and attractions.

If you are celibate, you know that you also have sexual attractions. Try telling God about them, again as concretely as you can. You, too, were created with sexual desires and attractions.

You can also talk with God about your feelings toward your body and your sexuality. Do you like your body, your looks? Is there something about your body or your looks that troubles you? Do you worry about being found attractive by others? Just begin to talk to God about your body and your sexuality and see how it goes. As you become more comfortable, you may find more and more to talk about.

Have you talked with God about your sexual orientation? Why not try it now. Just tell God about your sexual attractions. Don't let shame get in the way. We have not chosen our genetic makeup, our parents, the culture into which we were born, or the kind of upbringing we have had. As you open up with God, how do you feel? Do you get a sense of how God reacts?

Throughout history and even in the present, some people, perhaps more than we know, have experienced erotic and sexual arousal while in prayer. Recently a woman told me that she was disturbed at the erotic and sexual feelings that came up when she felt close to God. I suggested that she try telling God about her feelings and asking for God's response. When she tried this, she felt more at ease about her sexual feelings, sensing that they were somehow an integral part of her desire for God. So if you experience such feelings, why not try telling God the truth about them and see how God reacts. Remember that the Song of Solomon is in the Bible because the people of God felt that it expressed something about the relationship between God and his people.

More Difficult Issues

Now let's explore some more difficult issues using, as an example, one concrete case from the Bible. David, the king of Israel, was at home while his army was off on a campaign. He happened to be on the roof of his palace one afternoon when he saw a very beautiful woman taking her bath. He inquired about her and found out that she was Bathsheba, wife of Uriah the Hittite. David was strongly attracted to Bathsheba. (See 2 Samuel 11 for the details.) This story may remind you of some times when you were sexually attracted to someone and knew that the other person was morally off limits.

David impulsively acted on his desires, bringing Bathsheba into his house and engaging in a sexual relationship with her while Uriah was away with David's army. When Bathsheba became pregnant, David brought Uriah back to Jerusalem and tried to get him to sleep with her so that he would think the child was his—but to no avail. Finally, David sent Uriah back to the campaign with a letter telling the commander to put Uriah in a dangerous situation and allow him to be killed.

Now let's use this example to explore talking with God about sexual desires that may lead to actions that are illicit or sinful. Suppose that David had talked with God about his sexual attraction to Bathsheba. I suspect that if he had done so, he might have come to his senses. Let's explore the possibility of talking with God about sexual attractions that could lead to sin.

I know of people who have begun to talk with God about the sexual impulses that usually lead to masturbation. They tell God exactly what is going in their fantasies and bodies. When they do begin to talk with God, these impulses lose some of their force. They find themselves able to sleep after a sexual fantasy begins where before they believed that they could not do so without masturbating. Being open with God about our sexual desires and fantasies is another aspect of our growing friendship.

The same is true when we find ourselves, like David, sexually attracted to someone who is "off limits" because of one's own or the other's commitment or because the relationship is inappropriate for some other reason. We can tell God about the attraction. I don't mean telling God about how much we may dislike ourselves for having such attractions, but telling God about the attraction itself. David, for example, could have told God how lovely Bathsheba looked and how sexually attracted he was. When you feel such a sexual attraction, I encourage you to talk concretely with God about what is happening in your heart, mind, and body. Don't let shame keep you from being as honest and specific as you can be.

Are you finding these exercises, these ways of telling the truth to God, helpful and freeing? I hope so. If you are feeling more free and comfortable, you have something else to tell God. If you are more tense and nervous, you also have something to tell God. However, in this case I suggest that you seek out someone whom you trust and talk about your reactions to this chapter or any chapter of the book. Sometimes we need more than a book to be able to talk honestly with God about issues of sexuality and other matters.

11
Telling God about Your Sins

Think of what happens with a friend when one of you has hurt the other and you cannot talk about what has come between you. You become more careful with one another because at any moment the painful incident may intrude and the wound be reopened. Friendships begin to wither when offenses are not admitted and forgiven. I know of a father who stopped speaking with an adult son when the son married a woman of whom the father disapproved. Neither tried to mend the relationship until near the end of the father's life. Jesus had this to say about the need for talking openly about transgressions:

> If another member of the church sins against you, go and point out the fault when the two of you are alone. If the member listens to you, you have regained that one. But if you are not listened to, take one or two others along with you, so that every word may be confirmed by the evidence of two or three witnesses. If the member refuses to listen to them, tell it to the church; and if the offender

> refuses to listen even to the church, let such a one be to
> you as a Gentile and a tax-collector.
>
> —Matthew 18:15–17

Jesus knew how easily friends can hurt one another and that if the hurts are not dealt with openly and honestly, they can wreck friendship and a community.

The Unease of Silence and the Relief of Speaking

Our sins can get in the way of our friendship with God. In Psalm 32 David speaks not only of the relief of confession of sins but also of the unease brought on by silence.

> Happy are those whose transgression is forgiven,
>   whose sin is covered.
> Happy are those to whom the Lord imputes no iniquity,
>   and in whose spirit there is no deceit.
>
> While I kept silence, my body wasted away
>   through my groaning all day long.
> For day and night your hand was heavy upon me;
>   my strength was dried up as by the heat of summer.
>
> Then I acknowledged my sin to you,
>   and I did not hide my iniquity;
> I said, "I will confess my transgressions to the Lord,"
>   and you forgave the guilt of my sin. . . .
>
> You are a hiding place for me;
>   you preserve me from trouble;
>   you surround me with glad cries of deliverance.
>
> —Psalm 32:1–5, 7

We have already seen that a developing friendship with God can be short-circuited by shame. It can be short-circuited even more easily by our sense of sinfulness. When I become aware of how much I have fallen short of God's expectations, I may conclude that I am unworthy of God's friendship. Instead of talking with God about my feelings of shame and guilt, I may try to make up for my sins by doing good deeds or by going to Mass more. If something like this happens, then, once again, I fall back into a kind of insanity in which I become the arbiter of who God is. In effect, I believe that God can't want to be a friend of a sinner like me, but perhaps if I work hard at doing good, God will forgive me. We show our real beliefs by how we behave, not by what we say.

Our Human Reality

The reality is that all God's human friends are sinners. In a homily, the late Jesuit David Donovan noted that most organizations require some positive quality for membership, a high IQ for Mensa, Irish heritage for the Ancient Order of Hibernians, and so forth. The entrance requirement for Alcoholics Anonymous, on the other hand, is the statement, "I'm Jack, and I'm an alcoholic." He then went on to say that the entrance requirement for Christianity is similar, "I'm Jack, and I'm a sinner." The welcome mat is there for the whole human race, since every one of us, save Jesus and his mother, are able to say as much. If being a sinner were a hindrance to friendship, God would have very few friends indeed.

Being unwilling to admit our sinfulness to God, however, can get in the way. This is tantamount to being unwilling to face the truth about ourselves. Being a friend of God is demanding, just as any friendship is demanding.

Any deep friendship will reveal facets of myself that I don't want to face—for example, my selfishness, which shows itself in my reluctance to have my routines upset by a request from a close friend. The deeper a friendship gets, the more both parties' flaws of character come to light. Am I willing to allow my friend to know me at this depth and trust that our friendship will still last? Am I willing to ask my friend to let me know if something about me bothers him or her? Am I willing to be that vulnerable?

Sin as a Blind Spot

Well, the same thing goes for friendship with God. I cannot be God's friend and not face some of my sinful ways; God is truth as well as love. Some of these sinful ways will come clear to me only if I ask God to reveal them to me. I have a blind spot for my own sins and weaknesses; God and, perhaps, my closest friends see me more clearly than I do. Am I willing to speak with God about my sins and failings and to say as my own words what the psalmist says at the end of Psalm 139?

> Search me, O God, and know my heart;
>   test me and know my thoughts.
> See if there is any wicked way in me,
>   and lead me in the way everlasting.
>
> —Psalm 139:23–24

Here the psalmist trusts that God has only his good at heart; hence he is willing to ask God to reveal to him his sinful ways. People who have tried this exercise in trust have been amazed and relieved at how honest and forgiving God can be. As they begin to speak honestly with God about their past failures and sins, they see more and more clearly their real sinfulness. Often the deeper problem is not the sin upon which they've been focusing. For example, someone who is scrupulous may discover that the real sin was thinking that God is the kind of ogre who demands perfection in every detail. The alcoholic may realize that sinfulness lay, not so much in the overconsumption of alcohol, but in the unwillingness to admit his or her powerlessness to use alcohol moderately. As they face this reality, they sense God's loving embrace of forgiveness, and a great weight is lifted from their shoulders. With a sigh of relief and often with tears they thank God for such kindness and love. Perhaps you have experienced something like this in the sacrament of reconciliation after you have confessed your sins to the best of your ability and received absolution.

"But God Knows Everything"

Telling our sins to God may seem silly since "God knows everything." However, as noted earlier, it's not a matter of information, but of trust. By telling God our sins, and in detail, we get them off our chest and can experience God's response of forgiveness more deeply. It's what happens when we tell a good friend what we have done and ask forgiveness; a weight is lifted from our hearts. Those who make the *Spiritual Exercises* of Ignatius of Loyola are encouraged to ask God to open their eyes so that they can see the sinful patterns in their lives. Then they recall the various periods of their life trusting that God will show them where they have fallen short in each of those time periods. At the end of this meditation Ignatius proposes the following consideration:

> Exclamations of wonder, with intense feeling, as I reflect on the whole range of created beings, how ever have they let me live and kept me alive! The angels, who are the sword of divine justice, how have they endured me, and looked after me, and prayed for me! How have the saints been able to intercede and pray for me! And then the heavens, the sun, the moon, the stars and the elements, the fruits, the birds, the fishes and the animals, how have

they kept me alive till now! As for the earth, how has it not opened to engulf me, creating new hells where I might suffer for ever!

Colloquy. I will conclude with a colloquy about mercy. All my thoughts will be about mercy and I will thank God for giving me life up till now, proposing to do better in the future with His grace.

—Spiritual Exercises, n. 60–61

Before his conversion Ignatius had lived a rather loose life. So he must have felt the kind of wonder and gratitude he suggests as he allowed God to reveal his sins to him and realized that God still loved him. Have you ever tried this kind of exercise? When people do this exercise, they often compare their feeling of relief to having a great load lifted from their shoulders.

A Great Burden Is Lifted

The film *The Mission* tells the story of some Jesuits who worked with the Guarani tribe in South America in the sixteenth and seventeenth centuries. Robert de Niro plays a former soldier who had enslaved Guarani. Now repentant and a Jesuit himself, he chooses as his penance to carry his old armor and weapons on his back as the Jesuits climb to the site where the Guarani live. It is a very arduous climb. When they reach the top, a Guarani races with a machete toward him. You think that he will kill his former enemy, but instead he lops off the baggage, which drops behind de Niro into the gorge. De Niro begins to laugh and cry with relief, and the two embrace. That scene captures the relief of forgiveness when you know that the One who forgives knows you inside out.

One of the important spiritual disciplines toward sanity in Twelve Step programs comes with the fourth and fifth steps: "Made a searching and fearless moral inventory of ourselves" and "Admitted to God, to ourselves and to another human being the exact nature of our wrongs." Again, if you have ever participated either as an addict or as the other human being, you know that these steps lead to a great sense of relief and freedom.

The deepening of friendship with God never ends. Since both God and human beings are unfathomable mysteries, we will have a lifetime and all eternity to continue to learn about one another. You may be surprised that I lump human beings with God in being unfathomable mysteries. Yet we are created in the image and likeness of God. Of course, we are not the infinite mystery who is God, but we share in that mystery. Moreover, we are a mystery to ourselves. As we grow in intimacy with God, we find more of ourselves being brought to the surface. And we may be reluctant to reveal some of it to God. So the challenge of transparency, of truth telling, will always be with us.

12
Expressing Disagreement with God

Sometimes when I am praying or reading a psalm, I react negatively. Let me give you an example. At Night Prayer for Sundays, Psalm 91 is prayed.

> You who live in the shelter of the Most High,
>   who abide in the shadow of the Almighty,
> will say to the Lord, "My refuge and my fortress;
>   my God, in whom I trust."
> For he will deliver you from the snare of the fowler
>   and from the deadly pestilence;
> he will cover you with his pinions,
>   and under his wings you will find refuge;
>   his faithfulness is a shield and buckler.
> You will not fear the terror of the night,
>   or the arrow that flies by day,
> or the pestilence that stalks in darkness,
>   or the destruction that wastes at noonday.

> A thousand may fall at your side,
>   ten thousand at your right hand,
>   but it will not come near you.
> You will only look with your eyes
>   and see the punishment of the wicked.
>
> —Psalm 91:1–8

Taken at face value these words strike me as untrue. Jesus is a good example of a just person who was not protected from the arrows of misfortune. Many a good person has been cruelly treated without being saved by God from the cruelty. So I tell God that I don't believe this psalm. "I believe that you will save all of us as you did Jesus, but I don't believe that you keep us from all harm, at least as we understand harm. Innocent children and adults suffer horribly, and you do not intervene. Not only that, but I don't believe you will deflect the arrows from me or anyone else and let them hit someone else because you love me or the other person more. I don't believe you work that way. Am I right?" So far I have not heard that I am wrong.

Wrongheaded Prayers

A prayer that others find very helpful can strike me as wrongheaded. For example, years ago a friend gave me a prayer by a French Jesuit. It was entitled, *Prière de l'amitié*, "Prayer for Friendship." In the prayer I was supposed to ask God to grant that I might be true to my friends, but without their return of any affection or even common courtesy. It seemed to come down to this: I would be praying that I could be a good friend to others, but that I preferred that they not treat me as a friend; in fact, the prayer asked that they treat me badly. I surmised that the prayer was based on an understanding of what Ignatius asks for in the "third degree of humility," namely for the gift of being treated as Jesus was treated without sin on the part of anyone. Though at first intrigued by the prayer, I soon realized that I could not, in good conscience, pray it. It seemed to me a wrong-headed understanding of Ignatius. I told Jesus that I thought I would be asking for my friends to remain spiritual and human children so that I could become more like him; I did not think that he prayed like this to his Father. Jesus did not seem to tell me I was wrong.

One final example, and here I tread on delicate ground. I do not want to sound disrespectful to Our Lady, but it has to do with the Salve Regina (Hail, Holy Queen), the lovely prayer that ends the daily prayer of the church. The Latin has been set to a tune which I love to sing with others. However, at one time I began to think seriously about what I was saying. "Hail Holy Queen, Mother of mercy, our life, our sweetness and our hope." I said to Mary, "Jesus is my life and my hope; you are his mother and for that I am profoundly grateful to you. I love you a great deal, but you are not my life and hope. I hope that I am not offending you." I did not get the feeling that she was offended.

I mention these three examples to give you a chance to think of how you react when you do not agree with a prayer in the liturgy or in a prayer book. I have come to believe that these disagreements or discomforts are another facet of ourselves that we can reveal to God, fully expecting that God will receive our self-revelations with the respect and love of a friend and that God can show us we are wrong if we are.

Feeling That God Has Dealt Us a Bad Hand

The psalmists can disagree with God. Psalm 44, which we read earlier, is a good example. It is a prayer to God in a time of great distress for the people. Clearly the psalmist believes that the suffering is unjust, and he tells God so and practically demands that God act to save them. After telling God in some detail what the people had heard about God's help for the Israelites in the past, he begins to berate God for failing to protect the people now and then goes on to tell God that what has happened to them is undeserved.

> All this has come upon us,
>   yet we have not forgotten you,
>   or been false to your covenant.
> Our heart has not turned back,
>   nor have our steps departed from your way,
> yet you have broken us in the haunt of jackals,
>   and covered us with deep darkness.
>
> —Psalm 44:17–19

Perhaps the prevailing theology of the time took the line that suffering and defeat were signs that the people had fallen away from their covenant with God. The psalmist will have none of this. He says that they suffer precisely because they have been faithful. In effect, he accuses God of not being faithful to the covenant.

You may at times feel that God has dealt you a bad hand. Have you told God how you felt? Do you want to try it and see how God responds?

Telling God How to Be God

Abraham is known by both Jews and Muslims as a friend of God. No doubt one of the stories that led to this characterization is the following. God is leaving the meeting place by the oaks of Mamre to see whether Sodom and Gomorrah are as evil as reported. "The Lord said, 'Shall I hide from Abraham what I am about to do?' . . . No, for I have chosen him." (Genesis 18:17–18). So God tells Abraham about the proposed destruction of these cities. Abraham approaches God and says:

Will you indeed sweep away the righteous with the
wicked? Suppose there are fifty righteous within the city;
will you then sweep away the place and not forgive it for
the fifty righteous who are in it? Far be it from you to
do such a thing, to slay the righteous with the wicked,
so that the righteous fare as the wicked! Far be that from
you! Shall not the Judge of all the earth do what is just?

—vv. 23–25

Abraham tells God how to be God. That's how cheeky he
became in his friendship with God. How did God react? Read
the rest of the story in Genesis and enjoy the humorous
exchange that ensues as Abraham haggles with God about how
many righteous people it would take in Sodom and Gomorrah
to save the cities. Clearly the writer of this story thought that
God enjoyed Abraham's boldness in challenging God.

What is at stake here again is our willingness to tell God
the truth as we see it, with the hope that we will be proved
wrong—if we are wrong.

Doubts about Faith

If you are in any way like me, you have doubts about faith. Here,
too, honesty is the best policy for friendship with God. Sometimes it has occurred to me that God may be a creation of my
own need. We believers are part of this secular age in which, for
good or ill, faith is no longer taken for granted; we know good
and intelligent people who do not believe in God. It's no wonder that we have doubts at times, and perhaps often.

A young Jesuit was making the full thirty-day *Spiritual Exercises* of St. Ignatius. At one point he began to wonder whether
all this God talk was just a product of his imagination. I asked
him if he truly wanted to answer the question. It dawned on us
that the enemy of human nature was behind this question; the

purpose was not to arrive at an answer, but to keep him ruminating about the question. I said: "If it's all a product of your imagination, then you should just pack up and go home; if it's not, then the smartest thing you can do is to continue to pray." The enemy of human nature could not be more pleased than when we keep ruminating and never come to a decision one way or the other. Notice, too, that such questions keep us from conversing with God.

When I have doubts about God's existence or about some of the tenets of religion, I try to be honest with God about them. I tell him what I am thinking. What happens is that I realize ever more deeply that faith is just that: faith, not evidence. To believe means to put my trust in what is not seen. I have always ended such prayer with a deeper trust in the Mystery we call God and a sense that the Mystery is pleased with my honesty.

Disagreeing with Teaching Authority

We may disagree with teaching authority in the church, or at least question some of its pronouncements. When we find ourselves upset with or in disagreement with a particular teaching, we have something else to talk over with our friend. I find that such conversations give me some perspective on the matter at hand and also help me winnow out the essentials from the nonessentials in the teaching in question. Such prayer also helps me engage in conversation about such disputed questions with more compassion for those who disagree with me.

Whatever bothers us can be an occasion for prayer. God is interested in everything that troubles us and, I believe, enjoys our willingness to engage in frank conversation about touchy and controversial issues. Growth in friendship with God comes through honesty and truth telling on our part. The First Letter of John notes:

God is love, and those who abide in love abide in God, and God abides in them. Love has been perfected among us in this: that we may have boldness on the day of judgment, because as he is, so are we in this world. There is no fear in love, but perfect love casts out fear; for fear has to do with punishment, and whoever fears has not reached perfection in love. We love because he first loved us.

—1 John 4:16–19

I believe that God works overtime to convince us of this truth so that we will become the kind of friend Abraham and others became. Let's not be afraid to disagree with God, or least with what we think are God's "mistakes."

13
Thanking God

Thanking God is another way to tell the truth. Deep feelings of gratitude are the clearest proof, along with lack of fear, of our faith in God. After all, to believe in God is to believe that only God is God and that everything else that exists, myself included, exists only because of the generous bounty of God. In addition, belief in God entails belief that "all shall be well, and all manner of thing shall be well," as Julian of Norwich wrote centuries ago. What's not to be grateful for, if that's what we really believe!

Of course, most of the time we don't really believe this. We are unaware of our absolute dependence on God and thus blithely oblivious of the most important reality about us. We act as though the advertisements proclaiming that we deserve a good night's sleep, a fat bank account, good health, good abs, and so forth were true. When we live out of this kind of fantasy, we are unbelievers and out of touch with reality.

But when we do become aware of the reality of our utter dependence on God's goodness for every breath we take, then we have a chance to acknowledge that reality by thanking God.

Wake-Up Calls

Sometimes it takes a jolt to make us aware of how dependent we are on God's desire for us. We lose a loved one to illness, face a life-threatening illness, realize that we are too dependent on some substance for our own good and yet cannot give it up, get fired from a position upon which our livelihood and identity depend in some way. Some crisis forces us to face how precarious is our hold on existence. These moments of acute crisis can bring out the best or the worst in us; they can be a wake-up call to faith or lead to a downward spiral of depression, darkness, despair, or resentment. Most of us first go into the downward spiral before hitting some bottom and there find God waiting for us to lead us back to sanity. I have met many people who overflow with gratitude for such wake-up calls because they were brought back to God and found peace, serenity, and sanity.

Some of the psalms show such gratitude after, or even in the midst of, great difficulty. In Psalm 40, David tells of waiting for salvation and then giving thanks publicly for deliverance:

> I waited patiently for the Lord;
>   he inclined to me and heard my cry.
> He drew me up from the desolate pit,
>   out of the miry bog,
> and set my feet upon a rock,
>   making my steps secure.
> He put a new song in my mouth,
>   a song of praise to our God. . . .
>
> I have told the glad news of deliverance
>   in the great congregation;

see, I have not restrained my lips,
  as you know, O Lord.

—Psalm 40:1–3, 9

In our liturgies we often hear people thanking God publicly for graces received. It's a normal thing to thank God when we come through trial or tribulation. Through this crisis the psalmist has come to realize, perhaps not for the first or last time, that he is dependent on God *always*. Hence he ends the psalm, "I am poor and needy, but the Lord takes thought for me" (v. 17). His focus has shifted from himself to God. This is often what happens when we tell God the truth; something shifts inside, we feel heard and understood, and spontaneously we want to say thanks to the One who has listened to us.

In chapter 2 we met a hospital chaplain who felt overwhelmed and angry at the demands placed on her. As she was heading toward her unit, she told God how angry and put upon she felt; then she walked into the unit and was greeted with hope and warmth by the nurses. Her anger turned into great gratitude to God for this grace.

Occasions for Thanking God

Anniversaries give us a chance to give thanks to God for blessings received. As we recall the years of a marriage or of a particular occupation, we can be filled with gratitude for all the good that has come our way. My eight-day retreat in 2010 gave me the chance to reflect on sixty years as a Jesuit. I spent the days of the retreat revisiting with Jesus the various parts of those years and was at times rendered speechless with gratitude for all that God had done for me.

Robert Doherty, SJ, one of my friends and a seasoned spiritual director, suggests that people who are celebrating anniversaries make a psalm of gratitude for their salvation history. He points out that a number of the psalms are alphabetic in the Hebrew; the first verse or section of verses begins with a word starting with aleph, the second with a word starting with beth, and so on. (These psalms are 9, 10, 25, 34, 111, 112, 119, and 145.) He tells people that they can go through their life thanking God for the people and things beginning with *a*, then *b*, and so on. You can begin by asking God to help you to recall all the important events and people in your life or in your career or marriage or whatever it is you are celebrating. Then let the memories come, going from A to Z, and bless the God who has so abundantly blessed you.

Another way to give thanks is to use Psalm 136, a psalm of praise and thanksgiving with the repeated line "for his steadfast love endures forever." The psalmist goes through all that God has done for the people of Israel. Here is a short sample.

> O give thanks to the Lord, for he is good,
>   for his steadfast love endures forever.
> O give thanks to the God of gods,
>   for his steadfast love endures forever.
> O give thanks to the Lord of lords,
>   for his steadfast love endures forever;
>
> who alone does great wonders,
>   for his steadfast love endures forever;
> who by understanding made the heavens,
>   for his steadfast love endures forever;
> who spread out the earth on the waters,
>   for his steadfast love endures forever;
> who made the great lights,
>   for his steadfast love endures forever;
> the sun to rule over the day,
>   for his steadfast love endures forever;

the moon and stars to rule over the night,
　for his steadfast love endures forever.

　　　　　　　　　　　　　　　—Psalm 136:1–9

You could go through your whole life or a part of it using the refrain of this psalm over and over again, expressing thanks to God.

Does Our Gratitude Make Any Difference to God?

Does it matter to God that we are grateful? Recall the story of Jesus healing ten lepers, and only one, a Samaritan at that, came back to thank him. Jesus said on that occasion, "Were not ten made clean? But the other nine, where are they? Was none of them found to return and give praise to God except this foreigner?" (Luke 17:17–18). Apparently it matters to Jesus. But it can't be that Jesus or his Father are standing on protocol, demanding gratitude for favors granted. I believe that it matters to them because it's a matter of sanity for us. Ingratitude or the inability or unwillingness to say thanks flies in the face of the reality of who we are. We exist only by the gracious desire of God; so our reality is to be totally dependent on God; if we fail to see this reality, then we are insane. And God does not want us to live insane lives.

Such insanity leads to the feeling of entitlement that bedevils relationships between people. Such a feeling is the only explanation for the behavior of the slave in Jesus' parable who was forgiven a great debt and then went out and refused to forgive a much smaller debt owed to him (Matthew 18:23–35). He could act so outrageously only if he felt that he was entitled to the forgiveness of his great debt. Lack of gratitude leads to a sense that I deserve what I have and what I am. We forget that everything we have is unearned, and so we easily credit ourselves and fear that we will lose what we have to others if we are not careful.

Ingratitude too easily leads to a dog-eat-dog world in which each person cares for him/herself and lives in fear of others.

The poet Edward Hirsch was moved to "wild gratitude" one evening while playing with his cat and was reminded of the eighteenth-century English poet Christopher Smart, who spent his life thanking God for all the ordinary blessings of his life. Perhaps it will remind you of the simple pleasures and blessings of your own life.

Wild Gratitude

Tonight when I knelt down next to our cat, Zooey,
And put my fingers into her clean cat's mouth,
And rubbed her swollen belly that will never know kittens,
And watched her wiggle onto her side, pawing the air,
And listened to her solemn little squeals of delight,
I was thinking about the poet, Christopher Smart,
Who wanted to kneel down and pray without ceasing
In every one of the splintered London streets,

And was locked away in the madhouse at St. Luke's
With his sad religious mania, and his wild gratitude,
And his grave prayers for the other lunatics,
And his great love for his speckled cat, Jeoffrey.
All day today—August 13, 1983—I remembered how
Christopher Smart blessed this same day in August, 1759,
For its calm bravery and ordinary good conscience.

This was the day that he blessed the Postmaster General
"And all conveyancers of letters" for their warm humanity,
And the gardeners for their private benevolence
And intricate knowledge of the language of flowers,
And the milkmen for their universal human kindness.
This morning I understood that he loved to hear—

As I have heard—the soft clink of milk bottles
On the rickety stairs in the early morning,

And how terrible it must have seemed
When even this small pleasure was denied him.
But it wasn't until tonight when I knelt down
And slipped my hand into Zooey's waggling mouth
That I remembered how he'd called Jeoffry "The servant
Of the Living God duly and daily serving Him,"
And for the first time understood what it meant.
Because it wasn't until I saw my own cat
Whine and roll over on her fluffy back
That I realized how gratefully he had watched
Jeoffry fetch and carry his wooden cork
Across the grass in the wet garden, patiently
Jumping over a high stick, calmly sharpening
His claws on the woodpile, rubbing his nose
Against the nose of another cat, stretching, or
Slowly stalking his traditional enemy, the mouse,
A rodent, "a creature of great personal valour,"
And then dallying so much that his enemy escaped.

And only then did I understand
It is Jeoffry—and every creature like him—
Who can teach us to praise—purring
In their own language,
Wreathing themselves in the living fire. [12]

Hirsch and Christopher Smart paid attention to what was right before them long enough to be overcome with wild gratitude for all they had received. Hirsch himself, unlike Christopher Smart, may not know to whom he is singing praise, but he knows that praise and wild gratitude are the signs of a sane person.

In addition to the fact that God wants us to be sane, we could say that God delights in our gratitude just as any friend delights in the gratitude of a friend. Aren't you happy when a friend thanks you for something you have done for him or her? Doesn't it make you feel even closer to your friend? The mutuality of friendship means a mutuality of gratitude, and I believe that such mutuality is what God hopes for with us. So I sense that God is grateful to us when we accept the offer of friendship and are grateful for it.

On one of his annual retreats, a Jesuit friend, who has battled many health issues in his life and come close to death on more than one occasion, heard God express gratitude that he was willing to hang on, to continue to live. In a later prayer session, the man said jokingly, "You owe me big time." Almost immediately he thought of Job and humbly said to God, "You don't owe me anything," and cried. The next day he heard God say, "You don't owe me anything," and he cried some more.

The amazing thing about God's desire for our friendship is that God rejoices in and is grateful for our gratitude and happiness. The sisters of Notre Dame de Namur recall how their founder was fond of saying: *Ah! Qu'il est bon, le bon Dieu*: "Oh how good the good God is!" Amen!

14
What We Learn about God

Once when I was contemplating Jesus washing the feet of the disciples (John 13:1–5), I was stunned by the humility of God. From the beginning of his Gospel, John goes out of his way to insist that Jesus is God in human flesh. "In the beginning was the Word, and the Word was with God, and the Word was God. He was in the beginning with God. All things came into being through him, and without him not one thing came into being" (John 1:1–3). With this in mind, now read the following passage; God in human flesh acts this way.

> Now before the festival of the Passover, Jesus knew that his hour had come to depart from this world and go to the Father. Having loved his own who were in the world, he loved them to the end. The devil had already put it into the heart of Judas son of Simon Iscariot to betray him. And during supper Jesus, knowing that the Father had given all things into his hands, and that he had come from God and was going to God, got up from the table,

took off his outer robe, and tied a towel around himself.
Then he poured water into a basin and began to wash the
disciples' feet and to wipe them with the towel that was
tied around him.

—John 13:1–5

In the original Greek, the first four sentences of this translation
are one periodic sentence that stresses Jesus' self-knowledge and
his knowledge of his disciples, and the sentence ends with him
on his knees before them washing their feet. Among them is
Judas, who has decided to betray him. Condescension does not
quite describe what Jesus was doing. Rather, it was a great gesture of humility. Jesus knew who he was; he knew the kind of
men his disciples were; and that knowledge led him to this over-
whelming act of kindness, generosity, and humility. If we want
to know who God is, our best bet is to contemplate Jesus of
Nazareth. Here he shows us how humble God is.

If you have been praying with as much honesty as you can
muster, you likely have discovered certain things about God.
God humbly waits for us to pay attention; God is looking at
us, waiting for us to look back. God seems to be interested
in everything about us, even our petty concerns and worries.
We have explored telling God about our successes, our failures,
our worries and fears, our sadness, our envy and pettiness, our
anger, our sexual desires and attractions. As you have revealed
some of these facets of yourself, how did God respond? In those
responses God revealed Godself to you.

We have seen examples in the psalms and in ordinary life of
how God responds with concern and compassion, and at times
with humor, to our self-revelations. In the Bible we repeatedly
read that God hears the cry of the poor. He has heard our
cries, our joys, and our hopes, and we have been deeply con-
soled. In the process we have learned a great deal about God.

One of the ways doctrine develops in the Church is through the prayers of God's people. As we reveal ourselves to God, God reveals self to us, and in the process some of the distortions in our theology and spiritual practice are revealed for what they are—misunderstandings about who God is. I hope that some of your distorted images of God have been changed, as mine have been, by truth telling in prayer.

Years ago I asked my Irish-born mother what God was like for her. She replied quite simply, "He's a lot better than he's made out to be." A lifetime of prayer taught her something about God that did not square with a lot of the preaching she had heard. In a lifetime each of us will only dimly grasp the reality of God, but every time one of us gets God more right than before, that person contributes to the ongoing task of the Church to know God better in order to love God more and to engage with God more fully in the great work of creation. What a wonderful life!

15
Friendship with God Humanizes Us

This is a book about telling God the truth about ourselves. Here I want to reflect on how such truth telling humanizes us—that is, brings us closer to being images of God, adults in mind and heart who are able to help God attain the dream of the Peaceable Kingdom.

The Slow Growth to Becoming a Human Being

In her novel *Evensong* Gail Godwin tells the story of Margaret Gower Bonner, an Episcopal priest married to another priest. In one scene Margaret engages in a conversation about prayer over several evenings with Josie, a troubled adolescent. When Josie blurts out that the Bible is about telling us how to be good, Margaret says:

No, it's a record of a people keeping track of their relationship with God over a very long period of time. The amazing thing is, this constant accounting of yourself to an unseen other does make you change and grow. Sooner or later you become more conscious of what you're doing. People go through some pretty awful stages as they fumble toward what they're meant to be. As you put it, cruel and whiny. It takes a long while to complete the transformation from "eye-for-an-eye" sandbox whiner into a loving person—a lot of us never make it.[13]

Godwin makes my point quite well. If, over time, we keep telling God the truth about ourselves and listen for God's response, we will gradually become more like the God with whom we engage. We will become less self-centered and more loving and thus more human.

In *A Secular Age,* Charles Taylor makes an interesting observation and then a hypothesis, both of which seem to fit the message of this book. The observation: "But whether the propensity to violence is biological or metaphysical, this still leaves an enigma that any Christian understanding must explain: how can human nature as we know it be in the image of God?" In other words, since human beings are propelled to action, often enough, by sexual and aggressive energy, how are we images of God? He then continues with the hypothesis:

Here's a hypothesis from within a Christian perspective: humans are born out of the animal kingdom, to be guided by God; and the males (at least the males) with a powerful sex-drive, and lots of aggression. As far as this endowment is concerned, the usual evolutionary explanation could be the correct one. But being guided by God means some kind of transformation of these drives; not just their repression, or suppression, keeping the lid on them; but some real

> turning of them from within, conversion, so that all the
> energy now goes along with God; the love powers agape,
> the aggression turns into energy, straining to bring things
> back to God, the energy to combat evil.[14]

In other words, we are descended from the animal kingdom
and so are endowed with sexual and aggressive drives and other
instincts that are in need of guidance by God so that we may
grow into the human beings we are created to be. Becoming
an image of God requires more than following our instincts
because we are endowed with reason and will. We act not just
from instinct, but also from intention; we must learn to choose
how to act as human beings, as images of God. For this we need
God's guidance. Such guidance cannot be reduced to repression
or suppression of any of our impulses, including our sexual and
aggressive impulses; it seems to require their conversion to God's
purposes in creation.

We are not born into a world that is totally in tune with
God's purposes; our sexual and aggressive energies and other
instincts have been, as it were, hijacked by the enemy of human
nature for purposes other than God's. You might say that Genesis 3 tells the story of this hijacking of human energies. Human
beings have succumbed to the temptation of Satan. He has
drawn us to a mistrust of God; hence we have tried to use our
intelligence, our sexual and aggressive energies, and much else
to try to gain control of our lives, to save ourselves. Our deepest desire is to want what God wants, but that deepest desire
finds itself contending with other desires that have gained a
foothold in our hearts, desires at war with the kind of faith and
trust in God required to attain what God wants for us and the
whole world.

Our Instincts and Drives Are God-Given

Our animal nature with its instincts and drives is God-given. So our tendency to be ashamed of our animal nature, our bodily functions, for instance, is off the mark; we need not be ashamed of gifts given us by God to live in this world. We are images of God; our instincts and drives must be part of what God saw as "very good" (Genesis 1:31). Yet *unbridled* instincts and impulses are a threat to all that we hold dear; they can destroy families, communities, nations, and even our world as we know it. We have tried to control them through laws, cultural mores, games, repression, sublimation, drugs, religious indoctrination, psychotherapy, and so on, without notable effect. At times, these attempts to control our impulses and desires have led to rebellion against all attempts at control, with no better results for the human race or the planet. Whatever maturity we have achieved, Charles Taylor believes, has been through God's patient tutoring, rather than through our bungling attempts to put the lid on our impulses or to remove controls altogether. I wonder whether it is not time for us to try another route, a route that has not been tried on a large scale in the history of the world. I am referring to an attempt on our part to cooperate consciously with God's humanizing project by bringing *all* our impulses into a direct relationship with God. Let's reflect on what this might mean.

In this book we have been talking about what friendship with God entails for prayer. We have seen, I hope, that this friendship has to be built on telling the truth. I suggest that such truth telling might be a way for all of us to engage consciously with God's patient humanizing project.

Suppose we learned from an early age that we could tell God exactly how we are feeling with regard to *everything*, that God is interested in all our feelings, no matter what they are. We could tell God about feelings that we might not want to mention to our parents or best friends. We could tell God how angry we were, how we hated our sister or brother, for example, or how we wanted to smash another kid's toys (or smash the other kid!). We could tell God about our sexual curiosity and, as we grew conscious of them, our sexual attractions. We would have been taught that acting on these feelings was inappropriate or not in our best interests for now, but that having these feelings was part of growing up. And we would have been taught that God listens and will help us use these feelings for our own good and the good of others.

What I am suggesting is that as a church and society we take seriously that our human nature—in its entirety—is a gift of God, a gift that God will help us use for good. I leave it for experts in child development to suggest ways of helping parents and religious educators engage in such conversations with children.

Letting God Shape Us from the Inside Out

Most people who read this book have been brought up in a world that did not honor every aspect of being human. If you are like me, you have felt too ashamed of your impulses to speak openly about them to God. But it's never too late to start a new way of relating to God. We can begin to tell God, our friend, the truth about ourselves. We can, carefully at first, begin to speak as honestly as we can about our fears, our anger, and our sexuality, and then pay attention to how God responds. We can try to tell God how we feel, in as much detail as we can. This is what the psalmists do. They don't pull punches.

God wants to help us become the human beings we are created to be, bodily and spiritual beings who are empowered by God to live the way God would live in this world. Indeed, God wants to help us to become other Christs, "participants of the divine nature" (2 Peter 1:4) who join in God's great work of transforming our fallen world into the new heavens and the new earth begun with the life, death, and resurrection of Jesus. Our human nature, with its instincts and drives, is given by God to help us to become other Christs. Sexuality transformed by God becomes part of the human desire for that fullness of life that I have been describing as friendship with God, with all other human beings, and with the rest of nature; our attraction to God also has sexual and erotic components, as is made clear by the presence of the Song of Solomon in our sacred Scriptures. Aggression transformed through friendship with God moves us to combat all attempts to pull us away from this deepest desire of the human heart and of God's heart.

As Taylor puts it, God's educative project aims at conversion "so that all the energy now goes along with God." Transformed sexual energy powers charity (*agape* in the Greek), which is the love that defines who God is. We are enabled to love others as God loves them, for their sakes, not ours. Transformed aggressive energy helps us combat evil and all those structures, norms, and rules that run counter to what God intends in creation. None of our human instincts and drives is an enemy of God's intentions, but through the cultivation of friendship with God over a lifetime they can be harnessed to the divine love poured out into our hearts by the Holy Spirit.

So that God may do the job of educating us to become mature sons and daughters, we need to let God into the bone and marrow of our being, into the messiness that characterizes our inner lives. We cooperate with God's patient project by letting God in on all those aspects of our inner lives of which we are conscious. Trying to keep secret from God any aspect of ourselves—whether shameful or wonderful—hinders God's dream of us becoming *like God*, through and through.

16
God's Interest in Past Sins

Do not remember the former things,
  or consider the things of old.
I am about to do a new thing;
  now it springs forth, do you not perceive it?
                                    —Isaiah 43:18–19

God speaks this word to the people of Israel exiled to Babylon because of their sins. From these words we might conclude that God is not interested in the past or in the past sins of the Israelites, but in the present and future, the return from exile that God has already set in motion. Yet many of us spend a lot of time worrying about God's reactions to our past sins. Is God as interested as we often believe? And if God is interested, what's the nature of that interest?

God Seems Uninterested in Past Sins

When Isaiah saw the glory of God, he cried out, "Woe is me! I am lost, for I am a man of unclean lips, and I live among a people of unclean lips; yet my eyes have seen the King, the Lord of hosts!" (Isaiah 6:5). In Luke's account of Peter's call to discipleship, Jesus used Peter's fishing boat to preach to the crowd. Afterward he told Peter to launch out for some fishing—and they got a huge catch of fish. When Peter saw this, he dropped to his knees before Jesus and said, "Go away from me, Lord, for I am a sinful man!" (Luke 5:8). It seems that when we encounter God, our reflexive reaction is to remember our sins and to recoil. How does God react?

After Isaiah's fearful outburst, an angel flew toward him with a live coal and touched his mouth, declaring, "Now that this has touched your lips, your guilt has departed and your sin is blotted out" (Isaiah 6:7). The past, it seems, was obliterated by this gesture, since, to God's question, "Whom shall I send?" Isaiah immediately responded, "Here am I; send me!" (v. 8). In Luke's Gospel, Jesus ignored Peter's expression of sinfulness, inviting him instead to something new: "Do not be afraid; from now on you will be catching people" (Luke 5:10). With that, Peter seemed to forget his sinfulness and left everything behind to follow Jesus. It seems that God is not all that interested in the past, but in the present and what the present can yield for the future.

But . . .

These are not, however, the only biblical texts that refer to God's memory of the past. In the great revelation of Exodus 34 Moses heard God say,

> The Lord, the Lord, / a God merciful and gracious, / slow to anger, / and abounding in steadfast love and

faithfulness, / keeping steadfast love for the thousandth generation, / forgiving iniquity and transgression and sin, / yet by no means clearing the guilty, / but visiting the iniquity of the parents / upon the children and the children's children, / to the third and the fourth generation.

—Exodus 34:6–7

Here God clearly has an interest in past sins, to the point of punishing future generations for the sins of their ancestors. Moreover, Jesus, speaking of the final judgment, noted that God remembers both the good deeds of those who will be put on God's right hand and the evil deeds of those who will be put on the left (Matthew 25:31–46). So it seems that God is interested in the past.

Using individual texts from the Scriptures is not going to get us very far, at least if we are going to use texts honestly. So I want to approach this question from the angle of discernment of spirits, along the lines mentioned in chapter 2. There's a way to remember the past that is godly—as God remembers it—and a way that is not.

Ungodly Remembrance

For some years I have been seeing for spiritual direction a recovering alcoholic who genuinely wants to be holy. It has become clear to both of us that a certain way of remembering his past is not from God. When he remembers in this way, he is pulled toward self-loathing and despair; he forgets the love and forgiveness of God and wallows in his own misery. Mind you, when these bouts began, he had much to regret in his past, and the desire to confess his past sins seemed like an authentic call to repentance. In addition, his knowledge of Christian spirituality gave him plenty of tinder to feed the fire of his self-loathing. But the ungodliness of this kind of remembering showed its hand by its relentless self-absorption and its frightening pull toward darkness and despair. God, who wants us to have life in abundance, could not be the source of such movements of spirit. It took some time and a lot of prayer for this insight to sink in, but when it did, he began to experience much more joy in life. At present he generally enjoys prayer and life and exudes a sense of peace, but he can suddenly find himself pulled toward remembrance of his sinful past with similar consequences. Now, however, he can rather quickly recognize these pulls as the temptations they are and take evasive action.

Ignatius of Loyola noted that Satan is like a commander who wants to invade a town; he checks all the defenses to find the weakest link and attacks there. "In the same way the enemy of our human nature makes his rounds to inspect all our virtues, theological, cardinal, and moral, and where he finds us weakest and in greatest need as regards eternal salvation, there it is that he attacks and tries to take us" (*Spiritual Exercises*, n. 327). In the case of the recovering alcoholic, the weak spots are a skewed spiritual theology and a propensity to self-loathing and self-absorption. These weak spots never fully disappear; hence they are available for attack. Once they are recognized as points of vulnerability, however, the person can also notice how the enemy of human nature uses them for his own purposes. Often enough a simple prayer for help or a resolute "Begone, Satan" leads to peace of mind.

Godly Remembrance

Ignatius of Loyola also gives us an example of godly remembrance of sins in the exercise on our past history of sin, mentioned in chapter 11. In the presence of God we recall our history of sin, not to wallow in guilt and self-loathing, but to repent, to turn ourselves away from self-destruction and toward a more abundant life. We ask God to help us recall our sins and our sinful patterns for the sake of transformation. The purpose of this godly kind of remembrance is not self-loathing but amendment. With this kind of remembrance, we ask God's help to repent, to turn our lives around so that we are pointed in the right direction, toward the abundant life Jesus came to give us: "I came that they may have life, and have it abundantly" (John 10:10).

The Past Affects the Present

Here we have a clue as to how the past matters to God. It matters because it affects the present and the future. The great insight of Sigmund Freud and others in his field was that we carry our past into the present, and that this past often causes us trouble in the present. In addition, historians are fond of saying that those who ignore the past continue to make the same mistakes.

Unfortunately, knowledge of the past does not often lead to better decisions in the present. We know people who continue to shoot themselves in the foot and yet know exactly the past trauma that leads to this repetitive behavior. History, too, is filled with examples of people and nations knowledgeable about the past who continue to make the same mistakes. So knowledge of the past is no guarantee of improvement in our way of life.

A psychiatrist once told one of his clients, "Insight is the booby prize; transformation is what we're after." For him, and for all good therapists, the purpose of psychotherapy is not psychological archeology for its own sake, but a recovery of the past for the sake of a fuller life in the present and future. This psychiatrist's interest in the past parallels, I believe, God's interest in it. God is interested in our remembering the past so that we can be free of those elements of the past that limit our having abundant life.

God is not interested in the past precisely as past. The past cannot be undone; it happened. God is interested in the past insofar as it has repercussions in the present and future. The good and bad of the past do affect the present with consequences for the future. God's interest in the past is for the sake of transformation, of a change of heart in the present so that more of the future will be affected positively. God wants us to remember our past so that we can rejoice in the good and repent of the evil we have done. And repentance means a change of heart and direction that will affect the future. It seems that, in God's view, insight is the booby prize; transformation for the sake of the future is what God wants.

In a way, to believe in God is to believe in and to accept the possibility of forgiveness and transformation. Faith in God shows itself in how we act, not in what we say. God is interested in the direction of our universe and wants our cooperation in moving the universe toward the new heavens and new earth of which the resurrection of Jesus is the beginning and the promise. At every moment, therefore, God's Spirit is actively trying to move us toward such cooperation with God's intention. To believe in God, therefore, means to accept these movements of the Spirit and to align ourselves with God's dream for our world—which, in biblical language, is "the kingdom of God." Thus, belief in God is more about the present and the future than about the past. The past has relevance only because it has brought us to this present time. How we proceed from here is God's abiding interest.

The Sacrament of Reconciliation

What are the implications of past-present-future when we participate in the sacrament of reconciliation? We use this sacrament best when our confession of sin and our reconciliation with the Church lead to transformed lives. Transformed lives are free of the fetters of the past and, therefore, of self-hatred and shame. We are free to live without fear or at least with much reduced fear, as beloved children of God and as participants in God's family business, which is the transformation of our world. That is, I believe, God's only interest in our past sins.

During his months of prayer and fasting in Manresa, the recovering sinner Ignatius of Loyola entered a period of great scrupulosity—an obsession with his sinfulness. He made confession after confession of his past sins but could not come to peace. He continually worried that during confession he had forgotten to mention some past sin or some circumstance of a past sin. He became so distraught that he thought of committing suicide. Finally, he realized that this search for absolute certitude about having remembered everything about his past sins was a temptation, and he resolved never to confess these past sins again. With this resolve he found peace and hope and was able to move on to a life of joy and service, and eventually to the founding of the Society of Jesus. When he resolved not to confess past sins, he was taking a risk of faith that God was not interested in his past sins the way a banker would be interested in recovering every last cent of a debt. He believed that God's interest in his sins ended when Ignatius was freed for more abundant life for his own sake and for the sake of others. He lived his new faith in God, counting on God to welcome him home when he died, rather than worrying that God might point a finger, saying, "You forgot something." Once we have confessed as best we can and have begun to turn ourselves in the right direction, then it does appear that God forgets all about our sins. Our slate is wiped clean.[15]

What about the new heavens and the new earth promised with the resurrection of Jesus—will there be remembrance of past sins? In *The End of Memory* Miroslav Volf argues effectively that in the age to come memory of wrongs done will be "consigned to its proper place–nothingness." He writes, "What incredible power evil would have if once you had wronged someone, you, the person you had wronged, and God would remain permanently marked by it!" If God were to remember evil for all eternity, then God would be marked by it for all eternity, and our bliss would be marked as well. He concludes, "The reason for the non-remembrance of wrongs will be the same as its cause: Our minds will be rapt in the goodness of God and in the goodness of God's new world, and the memories of wrongs will wither away like plants without water."[16] His argument strikes a chord with me. How about you?

Does what I have written ring true to your own experience of God? If not, would you like to experience God as interested in your past sins only in terms of healing, transformation, and continued forward movement? If you want to know whether what I have written is true, you might ask Jesus about it and then listen to what comes next. Perhaps he will remind you of the story of the Prodigal Son he told in Luke 15. There the father welcomes back the wastrel into the family as a son and throws a party for his return.

Endnotes

1. William A. Barry, *A Friendship Like No Other: Experiencing God's Amazing Embrace* (Chicago: Loyola Press, 2008); *Changed Heart, Changed World: The Transforming Freedom of Friendship with God* (Chicago: Loyola Press, 2011).

2. Richard Russo, *That Old Cape Magic* (New York: Alfred A. Knopf, 2009), 168.

3. Ignatius of Loyola's *Spiritual Exercises*. Cf. Saint Ignatius of Loyola, *Personal Writings*, trans. and ed. Joseph A. Munitiz and Philip Endean (London and New York: Penguin Books, 1996). All citations of the *Exercises* are from this edition.

4. Julian of Norwich, *Revelations of Divine Love* (Short Text and Long Text), trans. Elizabeth Spearing (London and New York: Penguin Books, 1998), 24.

5. Sebastian Moore, *Let This Mind Be in You: The Quest for Identity through Oedipus to Christ* (Minneapolis, Chicago, New York: Winston Press, 1985).

6. John Carmody, *God Is No Illusion: Meditations on the End of Life* (Valley Forge, PA: Trinity Press International, 1997), 126.

7. Gerard Manley Hopkins, "I Wake and feel the fell of dark, not day," letter of June 25, 1883; "Comforter, where, where is your comforting?" in *Gerard Manley Hopkins*, The Oxford Authors, ed. Catherine Phillips (Oxford and New York: Oxford University Press, 1986), 166, 373, 167.

8. Etty Hillesum, *An Interrupted Life: The Diaries, 1941–43* and *Letters from Westerbork* (New York: Henry Holt, 1996), 178.

9. Gerard Manley Hopkins, "Thou art indeed just," in *Gerard Manley Hopkins*, The Oxford Authors, ed. Catherine Phillips (Oxford and New York: Oxford University Press, 1986), 183.

10. Stephen Yavorsky, "You Look at Them; I'll Look at You," *Human Development* 29 no. 2 (2008): 9–10.

11. Marvin H. Pope, *Song of Songs: A New Translation with Introduction and Commentary* in *The Anchor Bible* (vol. 7C) (Garden City, NY: Doubleday, 1977), 17.

12. Edward Hirsch, "Wild Gratitude," *The Living Fire: New and Selected Poems* (New York: Alfred A. Knopf, 2010), 57–58.

13. Gail Godwin, *Evensong: A Novel* (New York: Ballantine, 1999), 76.

14. Charles Taylor, *A Secular Age* (Cambridge, MA: Harvard University Press, 2007), 668.

15. For Ignatius of Loyola's scruples, cf. "Reminiscences" in *Personal Writings*, 22–24.

16. Miroslav Volf, *The End of Memory: Remembering Rightly in a Violent World* (Grand Rapids, MI: William B. Eerdmans, 2006), 214.

Also Available

G rounded in biblical tradition but with a clear focus on Ignatian spirituality, *A Friendship Like No Other* offers a fresh approach to becoming a friend of God. Eschewing the idea that God is a distant, solitary figure to be feared, renowned spiritual director William A. Barry, SJ, provides us with all the tools needed to become a friend of God.

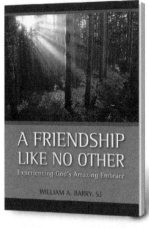

A FRIENDSHIP LIKE NO OTHER
Experiencing God's Amazing Embrace
WILLIAM A. BARRY, SJ

William A. Barry, SJ
$14.95 • pb • 2702-8

A Friendship Like No Other offers three well-supported and practical sections: prayerful exercises to help lead us to the conviction that God wants our friendship, a close look at objections to this idea, and reflections on experiencing the presence of God and discerning those experiences. Brief, personal meditations are woven throughout.

Also Available

In *Here's My Heart, Here's My Hand,* veteran spiritual director William A. Barry, SJ, helps us understand how we can experience a special friendship with God and what effects that relationship with God will have on our lives. Nearly 20 of Fr. Barry's finest previously published articles on the subject of friendship with God appear in this warmly written book. Although the selections are diverse in their overall themes—from changing our image of God to forgiving as Jesus forgives—each one shares the common thread of helping us see prayer as the way to a conscious relationship with God.

Here's My Heart,
Here's My Hand

Living Fully in Friendship with God

William A. Barry, SJ
$14.95 · pb · 2807-0

Also Available

Developing a friendship with God may be the starting point for the spiritual journey, but how can that important internal relationship move us to make an impact on—and even transform—the world around us?

In *Changed Heart, Changed World,* renowned spiritual director William A. Barry, SJ, delves into such topics as how friendship with God impacts our role in society, how to see forgiveness as a way of life, and how compassion can make its mark on the world. Throughout the book, Fr. Barry provides many practical ways to integrate the inner life, where we experience a relationship with God, with the outer life, where we live in relationship with our world.

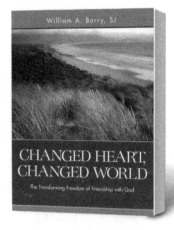

William A. Barry, SJ
$14.95 • pb • 3303-6

Also Available

What does it mean to have a relationship with God? Why do so many of us avoid a relationship with God at all costs? What examples from Scripture might guide us in developing a close, prayerful relationship with God? In *Seek My Face,* William A. Barry, SJ, provides thoughtful and easy-to-understand answers that can help anyone draw closer to God.

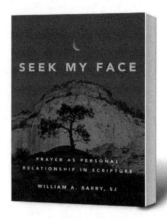

William A. Barry, SJ
$13.95 • pb • 2808-7

Throughout the book, Fr. Barry introduces situations and personalities from both the Old and New Testaments to show readers the various ways in which people in the Bible—Abraham, Moses, Peter—drew closer to God, and how we can use their examples to develop a closer relationship with God ourselves.